HAND ME THAT CORKSCREW, BACCHUS

HAND ME THAT CORKSCREW, BACCHUS

by

Mary Lester

THE PIPER COMPANY

Executive Offices
120 North Main Street
Blue Earth, Minn. 56013

West Coast Offices
P.O. 26274, U.S. Custom House
San Francisco, California 94126

Manufactured in the United States of America

International Standard Book Number: 0-87832-007-5

Library of Congress Catalog Number: 73-82326

First Edition, First Printing

To my marvelous mother, Clara Marie Lester, and to a man completely without guile — my handsome Jesuit priest brother, William F. Lester, S.J.

CONTENTS

HAND ME THAT CORKSCREW, BACCHUS

CHAPTER I

HOW IT ALL STARTED

I will never forget that conversation in the winter of 1961.

Louis Benoist called me in Miami to invite me into the world of wine, ending his conversation with the assurance that "everything will be taken care of."

For the next nine years everything was, in a gracious manner that seems to have disappeared in a world too busy to enjoy itself. And what a contrast from my former world. Until then most of my professional life had been spent working for newspapers. I felt journalism was the most exhilarating job on earth.

But I was to learn that there are other kinds of action. At Almadén I changed from a spectator, a journalist who isn't really a part of what she's covering, to a participant, a hostess who gave tours to a quarter of a million visitors at America's largest premium winery. I found more excitement than I had ever found before in the fascinating array of visitors that came to Almadén's door; in fact, it could be said the *world* came to me.

My world was at Almadén and its visitors my friends. Indeed my job was an event in itself, a never-ending succession of parties, tours, dinners or simple chats with visitors from halfway around the world one day and just down the road another.

The pell-mell rush of journalism wasn't in the job, but there was the contentment and enjoyment of work that capitalizes on one's sociability . . . and gives one champagne every day to ply it with.

I had been working with the Miami *Herald* for several years when it finally dawned on me that there was no future in it. The chances of my getting assignments I wanted — working the political or religious beat — were nil. So I began looking around.

It didn't take me long to see that there wasn't any public relations work in Miami that paid anything to drink about. Horace Greeley's "Go West!" wasn't uppermost in my mind, but the West did have a lure: a brother living there and the knowledge that the West pays better than the South.

In the fall I took my three-week vacation and flew to San Francisco to visit brother and job hunt. The trip was an immediate success. I'd been offered a job as a creative idea girl for an ad agency, which wasn't too much to my liking, but the agency vice president did phone an executive with the San Francisco *News-Call-Bulletin* to see about my working for that afternoon paper.

I've always had trouble looking mature enough to handle a responsible position, so I took pains to dress as sophisticatedly as possible: a black wool jersey with a straight skirt and a soft white mink collar. Before I grabbed a cab I thought it best to tone down my usual high-tensioned enthusiasm so I made a beeline for the hotel bar and had a cognac.

The upshot of it all was that the editor thought I would be good competition for the rival's long-standing political reporter. We reasoned that I could bring a fresh approach to reporting San Francisco's City Hall life. I was given two weeks to make up my mind about the offer and dutifully promised to respond from Miami within the prescribed time.

I'm glad he was relaxed enough not to press for a quick response, because I was elated at the offer. I rose to the full extent of my five-foot dignity, shook his hand, and ushered myself in a stately manner toward what I thought was the door to the City Room — and opened the door to the cloak and utility closet. Determined not to be shaken too easily, I grabbed a broom by the handle, curtsied and said: "Oh! Pardon me."

I've often wondered what the expression on the exec's face was; I didn't have the courage to look.

With two more days of my vacation left, I decided to

celebrate my good fortune, an easy task in San Francisco. I rang up an old newspaper friend and we decided a night on the town was in order. While we were enjoying a bottle of champagne, a waving hand from across the restaurant caught my attention. Although I hadn't the slightest idea who the man and woman were — I didn't have my glasses on — I waved back, smiled, and thought no more about it.

But a few moments later the maître d' brought over a note inviting us to join them. I still didn't know who they were, but then again you'll never meet anyone unless you respond to invitations — and besides they might be interesting.

Of course responding to *all* invitations can be a little risky. When one is very nearsighted — and unable to cope with contact lenses or a little too vain to wear glasses all the time — it is sometimes difficult to tell friend from foe. So, on the one hand, I always acknowledge a greeting and, on the other, I have had to learn when to be a little reserved. Like I had to learn not to leap into any car that happened to stop by a corner when I was waiting for a friend because it could be embarrassing and dangerous. It isn't that it could be the wrong person, but the wrong, wrong person. Still, I take my chances with a wave.

The couple whom we joined for drinks turned out to be one of *the* couples in the California wine industry. I had met them several times before but had not kept in touch. In a lovely postdinner conversation we discussed how California wines were making a strong run for the New York money. I promised to let them know as to whether I moved to California — fully expecting to — and thought nothing more about it.

A simple after-dinner talk and Eureka! Soon after my return from San Francisco, a Miami *Herald* switchboard operator said: "Long distance call for you, Mary." It was Ollie Goulet, the winemaster for Almadén Vineyards, asking me if I'd care to work for his company. Next on the line was his boss, Louis Benoist, the president of Almadén.

"How about it, Mary?"

Even though I had visited Almadén long before I was legally allowed to drink, working for one of the finest wineries in America was the farthest thing from my mind. So, naturally, I said the first thing that came to me, "Doing what? Pressing grapes?"

"No," Benoist answered, "you'd just sort of be helping us in Los Gatos." The "us" was his wife, Kay, and, I guessed, the winery. Normally, I'm not too logical a person, but still the brain cells were mystified; how could I work for the San Francisco paper and yet help "us"? The conversation went on for a few more minutes, but I hadn't yet figured out what I was supposed to do. I decided to end his expensive chat by reminding him that I doubted I'd be out to California to look over his winery for another few years because if I took the newspaper job that ended the winery job, and if I didn't (which was remote) it would take me that long to save enough to fly out again. Mr. Benoist couldn't see the problem. "I don't see why you can't come out for at least three or four days to look at the place."

"Does this mean you'll send me an airline ticket?" I asked, proud of myself because my thoughts were keeping up with everyone else's.

"Why of course, Mary, everything will be taken care of."

A couple of buddies switched their days off with me and within a week I was back in California; I had four days to "look at the place."

The plane trip was great excitement — three switches of airlines and an engine that conked out. Being an ex-airline stewardess, and a Catholic, I said the Act of Contrition and ordered another glass of champagne. The fact that the engine caught fire — on my side, yet — didn't ruffle me in the least. I noticed it had been "feathered" and kept right on turning the pages of *Life*.

But being three hours late did rile my host and hostess waiting for me at Almadén's main hacienda in Los Gatos. They're perfectionists, and their chef, Jimmy Hopkins, had prepared a superb meal to not only whet my appetite but to set me up, psychologically, for my stay. Since they had gone to that much trouble, it seemed perfectly in order to expect a DC-7 to do its part.

Ollie met me at the airport and an hour later I was being embraced by Kay and escorted into the sitting room, introduced to guests, shown the Anna Held guest bathroom, and immediately proffered a drink of my choosing. I decided my maladjusted tummy needed a cognac.

One of my favorite dishes is frogs' legs. One of Jimmy Hopkins' favorite dishes is frogs' legs. But by the time we sat down to the table that night my appetite really wanted nothing more than sleep. I nibbled and tried not to make it too obvious when I looked at my wristwatch as the minutes ticked away. It was after nine at Almadén and after midnight in Miami, but as I was soon to learn, the days and nights never end when one is with the Benoists and their guests — they are festive, fascinating and fun-loving, a continuous glass of champagne. And, as I was also to learn, after I'd returned to Miami, those three days there had an added feature: I was center stage, I was being watched closely to see how I reacted among doctors, lawyers, merchants and, I'm certain, thieves in the financial world.

It was a fiesta, a "happening," a Mardi Gras with the most sophisticated visitors in constant attendance. I thought it was just the Benoists' way of entertaining and tried not to feel the effects of too much champagne, slept as soundly as possible, faithfully did my exercises each morning and started in again each day.

Their object was to find out more than whether I could hold my alcohol or not and keep up my end of a conversation, whether interesting or boring. It was to also see if I tried to seduce or be seduced by every good-looking, influential male who came around. My job was going to be one requiring responsibility and a discreet nature; I would have to entertain an international society of friends and businessmen.

I survived. Looking back on it I'm not sure how, but I was young and fascinated by three days of partying, hardly aware that an interview was even taking place. I was overcome by my hosts' graciousness and by the stream of their celebrated and amusing friends. When I flew home I almost didn't need the services of the DC-7.

The word had been, "We'll let you know how you can fit in." I figured I had it made, so I wrote a "sorry, no" letter to the *News-Call-Bulletin* and began thinking California. But I didn't realize I was still being evaluated; the weeks passed and I began wondering if the newspaper would accept a somewhat abject political reporter.

Once again the Miami *Herald* operator said, "Long distance for you, Mary."

The voice on the other end ended my five-week frustration. "How long before you can come out here?" Louie Benoist asked.

"Six weeks," I answered, thinking of the round of parties I wanted to give and attend before saying goodby to my Florida friends.

"We'll have everything ready for your arrival." Again, everything was to be taken care of.

Six weeks later, to the day, I arrived at San Francisco International Airport, this time with the anticipation that a new job brings, not the anticipation of looking for one.

Within two years a job that had me baffled as to what to expect, but that sounded interesting and challenging, had become a career and a *first*; I was the first woman tour director in the wine industry. I had no way of knowing I would spend seven more years meeting thousands of interesting people, hundreds of top drawer VIPs, drinking wines from all over the world and learning secrets of the industry from the finest in the business, nursing my joy of drinking champagne and classifying hangovers as either A, B, or C.

In 1961, wine was just beginning to make its way into everyone's home. It was no longer thought of as something you ordered, with great hesitation, when you went out to dinner. As a leader in this movement, Almadén was no bungalow operation. My home was a hundred-year-old cottage that had formerly housed the winemaker. My backyard was two acres of grass, clipped hedges, rose bushes, half-barrels filled with colorful flowers, and two enormous gnarled oak trees which were acorns about the time the wood was cut for the house.

My front yard was five acres of concrete courtyard outlined by more hedges, flowers, and, dead center and almost directly in front of my porch, an island of trees and ivy. Other oak, pepper and horse chestnut trees were about. All of this plus acres of vineyards. It was a pretty setting.

One of the first items I remember was that all the trees were whitewashed from their bases to about three feet up the trunk. The white made magnificent markers when conditions were overcast and driving was hazardous, and it kept off some of the insects. I learned a little more about my boss when he expressed annoyance that the two-foot height limit he had ordered for the whitewash couldn't be maintained. The trees insisted upon growing and the whitewash went right along with the plan. Being an ex-Navy officer, Mr. Benoist liked things in order, including nature.

To the left of my cottage was a small parcel of vineyard and to its right was the winery — four square acres of it on the ground level. This was the 1876 plant, the center of operations and bottling. Across the courtyard was the original winery, built in 1852 at a time when most of California's settlers were far more interested in gold. The 1852 winery is still used for aging and offices. Across and to the right from the cottage was the original Almadén house, built in 1847, where the Benoists lived when they were in the area — and where their servants lived in near luxury.

In our little cottage my mother and I soon began to feel that, like the moss and ivy, we would become a part of the premises. However, the feeling didn't come as soon as we passed the gates. It took me three months to sleep through the night without waking; I was used to the noise of a city and not country silence, punctuated only by quail conversation, owl hoots (we had two permanent ones — the larger I named Oliver), and doves, as well as an occasional wine tanker coming in with its liquid cargo from the main vineyards at Paicines, to the south.

There were other adjustments. I had seen a skunk before because a friend kept one as a pet, but I'd never met one with all its accouterments. I smelled Sammy long before I met him. He sensed I wouldn't hurt him and burrowed beneath my cottage, where he made his home most of the time until Almadén's ever-increasing size drove him away.

For several years a family of 'possums hung around the cellars of the 1876 winery, scaring newcomers on the night shift who came unexpectedly across pairs of eyes staring at them as the creatures hung from the beams by their long, skinny tails.

Although I wasn't a farm girl, I was beginning to get used to the fauna. The cottontails, quail and partridge amused me, but the bugs, insects, snails, garter snakes and frogs had me jumping and scratching. I can't share the late Doctor Schweitzer's feeling that bugs have a soul; I step on them. For years if spiders or beetles remained somewhat stationary and there wasn't anyone else around to play executioner, I'd drop a telephone book on them. Someone else had to remove the weapon and the corpse. But after a little country exposure, if a spider wasn't big enough to carry off my antique chair he got the Raid gun; if he was big enough to move it, there was always my Luger.

Louie Benoist had his own style of humor. Once he displayed it while showing guests around the dark, damp cellars of the 1852 winery (dug deep into the earth to keep the wines cool). The cellar could easily have been the setting for Poe's "The Cask of Amontillado" with its moss growing between the hand-placed stone blocks. Besides the wine, it featured frogs about the size of a quarter, but with a terrific bark and always leaping about. I was often afraid I might step on one of them, or worse still, one would jump on me, so I avoided giving tours down there whenever possible. But duty called. So with the boss in tow I gingerly held my skirt about my legs with one hand and a glass of champagne in the other as I led the guests through the cellar. Mr. Benoist noticed my maneuverings but didn't say anything. There was just the slightest smile on his face as he glanced at me. Finally he couldn't contain himself any longer and asked in an offhand way, "What's wrong, Mary? Drafty?"

"No, Mr. Benoist, but I'm afraid of these ghastly little frogs jumping about."

"Don't worry, they always leap sideways," he said, turning away to pay attention to the conversation of his guests. The retort so amused me, and made me so conscious in a humorous way of my silliness, that the frogs never bothered me again.

I admit, however, to some confusion about my job at first. I soon began learning the names of the key employees and my way around the plant. I had two sets of personalities to consider, those of the rest of the employees, and that of Louie Benoist. First off, I didn't know what he wanted me to do. All he could tell me was that I would serve as a hostess for him and the missus when they were staying elsewhere, either at one of their other four homes in California, in Europe, or anyplace in between they decided to visit.

The job was a little more than saying: "How do you do?" and "May I get you another drink?" Three other girls had taken it on in the previous five years; one made it through seven weeks, another lasted three years. But personality clashes always arose. Actually there's really no problem working for the Benoists; they're wonderful. All you have to adjust yourself to is excitement, anything but ordinary working days, and irregular hours, not to mention one rule today and a change tomorrow. Like all folk born to wealth they have their eccentricities, but I hadn't worked a newspaperwoman's life for nothing: holidays off were unusual and the routine was always the unexpected. I'd get bored in any other situation.

When I came to Almadén that first winter there was no tour business. If a visitor showed up at the office and wanted to go through, someone who didn't look busy gave him a walk through the place. It was only the VIPs of the wine retail and wholesale field who were given a tour. If they were friends of the Benoists they usually entertained them. Otherwise, the wine buyers, restaurant owners and reps from the chain stores were shown around by the company's vice president and general manager, H. Peter Jurgens, or one of his staff from the sales department in San Francisco.

It was Ollie Goulet who decided I should learn about the business and give an occasional tour. An instant, "Oh! Yes!" put me on a five-month, self-taught course on the wine world. I stopped my social life and read over seventy books on wine (most of them dull), dozens and dozens of pamphlets, spoke with every winemaker I could collar, visited with viticulturists, wine chemists and winery personnel, and asked and wrote down the answers to hundreds of questions. I'm still learning.

After two weeks I gave my first faltering tour. In another two weeks I became connected with the sales department. Two or three groups had wandered in and asked for a tour. I gave them my best and they considered the tour informative, interesting and humorous and, unbeknownst to me, they reported back to H. Peter in San Francisco. He decided it was time to watch this new gal in action so he assigned a salesman, acting as spy, to observe one of my tours. The review was favorable and he was convinced my services would be valuable for handling the various wine VIPs that visited Almadén, rather than always diverting a salesman from San Francisco.

It was flattering to know he trusted me with the tours, especially since it would be several months before I actually met the six-foot-three, bronzed (thanks to the sun deck and sun lamps at the Olympic Club) working head of the winery. This blue-eyed, blond marvel of a man met with my instantaneous approval; he looked like the masthead off a Viking ship, and conducted himself in the same overpowering way. Through the years I was to hear many swear at him and by him, but I'm happy for a continued friendship — and also for the fact that our chances for falling out were slim since I saw him only four or five times each year. (I also learned how to stay out of telephone reach when necessary.)

H. Peter was and is a giant in the industry. He and Benoist had been of paramount importance in putting Almadén onto the sales map and into the White House. (When President John F. Kennedy was inaugurated, he chose Almadén Blanc de Blancs champagne for the celebration.) H. Peter later became President of the company and is now Chairman of the Board of the Wine Institute, headquartered in San Francisco.

The only thing I regretted about my first month at Almadén was the note of tragedy that struck soon after my arrival. I had just returned from shopping and lunch with Helen Goulet, the winemaster's wife, when she called to ask if my brother, a Jesuit priest, could be located. She wanted the two of us to come to Gilroy, some thirty-five miles south, where her husband lay seriously injured in the hospital.

In my company car, with less than a hundred miles on it, we sped rapidly toward the hospital, but what we didn't know, and what Helen hadn't been told, was that Ollie was dead on arrival from a collision with a Southern Pacific train. He had been on his way home to San Jose for dinner from the Paicines vineyards, which are located near Monterey, when he met the train on a spur track. One of his sons, returning from the vineyard just minutes later, stopped at the scene of the crash and identified his father.

So ended the life of a beloved man and fine winemaker who had started Almadén wines well on the road to popularity. Ollie had learned wine making while a Jesuit Brother at the Novitiate winery. When he decided being a member of a religious order was not his calling, simultaneously Louie Benoist was buying the then dormant Almadén winery and looking for a good winemaker. Mutual friends introduced them. The two men complemented each other in personalities and talents: Louie stating the quality of wines he wanted and Ollie formulating the ideas into reality.

After the funeral I questioned what would happen now that the winemaster was gone. The Benoists, on their way to Europe for a fortnight, returned from New York and faced the fact that their number one man at the plant and vineyards was dead.

There were changes, but Ollie had laid such fine groundwork that neither the wines nor his people floundered.

CHAPTER II

THE FIRST DAYS: BOOKS, BROWNIES, BIRDS

Since the death of Almadén's winemaster, Ollie Goulet, came shortly after my arrival, the next few months for me were filled with uncertainty. Would I find myself down at the state's unemployment office filling out the forms that asked: "What are you good at?" or, would I be able to hold onto the tiny niche I had made for myself, enlarge it, and make the job secure?

Ollie had run the entire operation of the winery. He gave his nod to every production move and to the hiring of every employee. A "no" from Ollie meant just that. Louie Benoist listened to Ollie carefully, regarded his opinions highly and almost always followed through with his suggestions. Ollie was *the* ruler of the vineyards and the winery and no one ever forgot it more than once.

From the first I had many things going for me. I like people and they like me. I entertain old friends, make them feel comfortable and welcome once again, and I make new friends into old friends quickly. I also had more than a beginner's knowledge of wine. (Besides, I actually drank wine, which put me in the minority.) But I had never lived on a vineyard and I knew next to nothing about the making and selling of premium wines.

21

So the first year was hectic. There was my cram course in learning everything about wines; much of it was done without the help of Ollie since he had died so soon after I came. But all the years at Almadén were hectic — the first year just introduced me to the "normal" life on that vineyard. The hours had long since passed sixty a week and had stretched to more tiring twelve- and fourteen-hour days — every day. But I didn't find it that difficult to get into the routine of long hours, just as I didn't find it difficult to keep sipping champagne.

Since nobody really knew what my job was supposed to entail, I had the run of the place and I soon found myself helping just about everyone who needed help and that's how I got to know so much about the workings of a winery!

My predecessors had been at Almadén mainly to entertain friends of the Benoists. But things had changed. First, I wasn't like the other girls; I wanted to do more. And second, the winery had grown. When I arrived it was already one of the largest quality wineries in California. But it was producing only about fifteen percent of today's yield. Most of the four thousand acres of top varietal vines then at Paicines were too immature to be picked (it takes about four years for vines to reach production status) and it wasn't until about 1965 that the fantastic supply of wines began to be noticed on the sales charts.

I took the lead in playing hostess to the Benoists' personal friends and business acquaintances, as I should have, but I also began helping the sales department entertain, showing "walk-in" visitors (civilians, we called them) around the winery and giving special tours for all sorts of VIPs. One touch that I found important was answering queries and writing letters and notes to people who had visited the cellars or who planned to.

Naturally one didn't give the same tour to Brownies and fourth graders that one gave to those over twenty-one, and especially, those over twenty-one who were already interested, either professionally or not, in wine. After a couple of years my time became so precious that I had to begin limiting the number of tours I could give to schoolchildren — in fact, without some extra help and an appointment book I could easily have turned the whole affair into an extra school class for the youngsters (there were about ten zillion of them in Santa Clara County) because there were so many requests.

I have fond memories of some of the groups, particularly

the students of one pretty, young teacher, Louise Pedrozzini, who sent her class's thank-you notes to me stuffed in a manila envelope. They included a variety of sensations about Almadén . . . and some pretty good art work, too.

One youngster from this fourth grade class at Oster School in San Jose said:

> Dear Miss Lester,
>   Thank you for letting us come to the Almaden Winery. We do thank you for telling us how long the wine has to be aged, and how old the winery is. We think the wine you make is probably very good. We enjoyed seeing all the awards you won. Thank you for taking us down into the old, old winery. Some of us were really scared . . . .

Another youngster wasn't scared, but her nose was active:

> Dear Miss Mary Lester, Winery Hostess,
>   Thank you very much for showing are class the Almadin wineery. When are class went to see the wine it smelled good.
>   I like your besent [pheasant] farm. The besants looked pretty. I was a child that took a lemon from the bushs. When we got on the bus and back to school, for lunch I ate my lemon, it was very good.
>   Thank you very much again, for showing us the Almadin wineery.

Another asked for a job:

> Dear Miss Lester,
>   Thank you for takeing us through your vineyards. Your homes are butaful. When I grow up I will be a truck and tack your nice wine all over the world four you.

Still another thought the winery interesting, but wasn't sure about the smell and prized our citrus:

> Dear Miss Lester,
>   Thank you for leting our class come to the winery. The winery was very interesting. I did not care for the smell. But after awhile I got used to the smell of the wine and the wood mixed together. Thank you very much. All of us picked your lemons. I hope no one picks anymore of your lemons.

One thing I hadn't anticipated when I began work at Almadén was that I was destined to become the Birdwoman of Los Gatos.

The Benoist home at Almadén fronted about twenty acres, part of which was taken up by a beautiful lawn on which croquet was sometimes played. Since Mr. Benoist expected nature to be always at its best, he couldn't stand the spots of brown that appeared on the lawn during winter, so he ordered them sprayed green. I always hated this unnatural blue-green look, but from a distance, like sitting on the verandah or relaxing on the patio, the lawn did have an even color about it — particularly while drinking.

The lawn was bordered by formal gardens on each side, thanks to the careful planning of famed landscape architect Thomas Church. Behind one of them were flower beds that gave us fresh blossoms the year around and behind another were a few acres of citrus trees, a vegetable garden and a small herb garden.

Further back still was a field where horses were kept, their barns and tack rooms, and coops for chickens, quail and partridge. Country living was hard to take . . . .

Before buying Paicines, the Benoists wanted to make their Los Gatos ranch home and the adjoining acres into their own personalized version of a French or English country estate. Their good taste led them to choose and direct the right people and they succeeded beautifully. So beautifully that *Sunset* Magazine called the gardens magnificent and the *cognoscenti* of the international set were unanimous: the estate was one of the loveliest in America.

What estate could be complete without pheasants? Some might say, "Why not peacocks?" but what with their screaming and molting they were too much for the Benoists — especially since the timing of their raucous screeches couldn't be controlled — and that wouldn't fit into the scene of lawns sprayed green or trees with the bases painted white to a prescribed height. Peacocks were out.

But pheasants were in.

One afternoon at lunch, Mr. B casually began saying that he wondered just what kind of pheasants he had — not merely what species they were, but much more about them. Their cages were run-down and he thought something should be done. All of this came out as simple conversation over dessert, but it hadn't taken me long to learn that casual conversation was not to be taken casually.

So I was paying attention to what he had to say, although I wasn't jumping into anything. I might as well have. Turning to me he asked, "Do you know anything about birds, Mary?"

"A little bit, Mr. Benoist." (In truth, the difference between a sparrow and a hummingbird, little more.)

"Well, then, find out what I have and get the cages fixed up and put signs up classifying the birds and see about getting some more. And, by the way, see if you can find out where we can buy some more quail and partridge. Kay says the ones we have now are too old and tough for eating. I had one last week and I agree."

Within a year I was an amateur ornithologist.

First I went bird counting. I felt like I ought to be wearing tweeds and a double-billed cap and holding binoculars. But a sweater and a pair of slacks would have to do. I took a few notes on what the pheasants looked like and then headed for the library to begin looking through pages of colored pictures of pheasants, trying to match what the Audubon Society showed with what we had in our pens. It took me hours to identify each one, partly because I liked thumbing through the pictures, whether they were helpful or not.

I discovered we had a very ordinary collection, and what's more most of the poor dears were mismatched in the cages. Unlike *homo sapiens*, birds want their own kind.

Thus began a hunt for a pheasant authority within a hurry-come-hither! distance. A dozen phone calls led me to one of the finest authorities on birds in the world, Lee Poisal. Lee had just retired from overseeing the world's feathered flock and had bought a small parcel of land near Livermore to raise some of the elite birds of the world (no pun intended).

Lee's help turned Almadén into the home of one of the finest private collections of rare birds in the United States. Since it was not the norm of Almadén to start anything slowly, within months the vineyards became the nesting place of thousands of dollars worth of fluttering friends.

San Jose *Mercury* Staff Writer Betty Barnacle wrote, "Often with a glass of their good wine, the Benoists serve a delicate bird, raised on the grounds. One can be sure it is always partridge. Benoist's pheasants keep their feathers."

And since I had walked smack into it, I became the chief

custodian of the birds. With Lee's help I made out diets, read up on possible illnesses, instructed the gardener-handyman when and what to feed, how to keep the cages clean, which eggs to gather and which to leave alone and how to make nests for those who didn't know how to shift for themselves (and learned the origins of the term *birdbrain*). I became an expert on perches and hutches and special diets, administering the latter to the point that the birds knew me as their featherless friend.

I became so attached to some of them that being awakened by Torres, the gardener, who suddenly found himself keeper of the cages, at 5:00 A.M. with an excited, "*¡Señorita, es necesario para usted visitar!*" didn't even put me in a lousy mood for the rest of the day. Normally the only thing I want at 5:00 A.M. is more hours of sleep, and having to get out of bed then puts me in such a mental funk that it takes hours before I'm with it.

Together, Torres and I went through the agony of watching Cicero, the Argus male pheasant, breathe his last in the wee hours. There was nothing we could do. He was three years old, had tail feathers up to a foot and a half long and three and a half feet around when spread. Most people swore he was a peacock. He and his mate, Minerva, had cost $3,800. There were, at that time, only three pairs of Argus pheasants in the United States. The San Diego Zoo had a male but no hen.

At a decent hour I called Lee and after listening to the facts he drove over to pick up the bird and performed an autopsy. The healthy, but stupid, bird had been frightened by an owl or maybe a barking dog and had flown from his perch in the dead of night in a panic straight into the overhanging metal grain container, breaking his neck.

We had been expecting Minerva to lay an egg for some time, which is a big event for an Argus — and for us, I might add — because they must be two to three years old before laying and will give only one egg a year. An Argus egg is worth fifty dollars as soon as it hits ground (no nest needed), assuming it is fertilized. If it isn't, it makes a very small breakfast and nothing more.

Four days after Cicero's demise, Minerva laid an egg.

Lee looked it over and decided we had breakfast and nothing more, so soon after we gave Minerva to the San Diego Zoo so the Argus population might be increased.

For quite awhile we let a few of the pheasants, notably the

Goldens and Silvers, out of their cages because they could be trusted to stay around, as long as food was nearby. The guests gloried in them as they preened and meandered about. But two were run over by wine tankers and three were taken by schoolboy neighbors, so back in the cages they went.

Except for one breed, the Blue-eared Manchurians, the poor little hens were a nondescript lot. If they could crow, they wouldn't have anything to crow about. But some of the males! They were so vain that during late summer and early fall, when it came time to shed their bright tail feathers and when their colors dimmed, they actually hid when anyone came to look at them.

Shortly after Almadén was sold to National Distillers in June, 1967, the powers that be in New York couldn't see any connection with birds and wine, so the order was to sell the lot. Like many items, I found that what someone had told you the birds were worth and how much someone else was willing to pay for them were two different stories. So I convinced management it would be just as well to donate the collection to the San Francisco Zoo; the company could get a tax write-off and at the same time "graciously" donate part of an estate that has never been the same since.

I had become so accustomed to the birds that I decided to keep some for my own when they had to be removed to San Francisco.

With Lee's help I had a large cage built and purchased several birds who could get along with each other, and until I left Almadén I continued to enjoy their trills in my own feathered fantasy of nature. The amount of care the birds required was minimal compared with the enjoyment they gave me.

There were some amusing sides to being an amateur ornithologist that didn't have so much to do with the birds as with everything that went into keeping them happy. Naturally our guests were overwhelmed by the sight of so many precious pheasants, quail and partridge, especially considering that together they were worth more than most of the guests were.

But these prima donnas were fed the simplest of meals. In fact, some of the birds had taken to Friskies Puppy Food and I finally decided to write a love-your-product letter to the president of the company. But to my surprise I never got so much as an acknowledgement. Since I kept a copy of the letter,

I reread it and felt the president probably thought I was being sarcastic. I wasn't; in fact I still use Friskies for my pets. At any rate, here's the letter:

President
Friskies Puppy Food
Box 260
Pico Rivera, Calif.   July 1, 1968

Dear Sir,
    For the past year and a half, I've been going to write you. That was when I started using your marvelous puppy food. In fact, one time I was going to send in the box tops to help support the Olympic Team, but I decided to give up on that unless I delivered them in person by truck!
    Hold on now, I use your puppy food for the birds in my aviary! Up until a few months ago, here on the grounds of Almaden we had one of the largest private collections of exotic birds in the United States. Since I ended up being buyer, dietician, and so on, I had to learn fast the favorite foods of those expensive friends.
    A top ornithologist told me that the Tutons and Emerald Green Tucanetts adored puppy food soaked down in water. So, each morning into the cages I'd wander, wearing a one hundred dollar dress and a fifty dollar pair of shoes, and mix the food for these particular birds. And I'm sure the visitors thought I was a "rare" bird as well! Anyway, there were certain birds who would eat nothing else but Friskies and fresh fruit.
    This January, we gave our aviary to the San Francisco Zoo. But I'm now hooked on these beautiful creatures and bought seven from my ornithologist friend. Some of these exist on Friskies. They are a pair of Bulbos from India and Thailand and one bird called "San," short for San Francisco, because his official title is: The Fairy Bluebird from Thailand. I even took pictures of the birds eating, but I should have placed your puppy food box next to their feeding pen.
    What I really want you to know, sir, is that in case any competitor makes disparaging remarks about your product, you can laughingly, as well as seriously, reply that Friskies is not only dog food, but also, for the birds!

                              Cordially,
                              Mary Lester

CHAPTER III

TOURING: GENERAL AND SPECIAL

How anyone could arrive at the winery before 11:00 A.M. and start drinking was a mystery to me. I suppose free champagne accounts for it.

But entertaining visitors with tours was my job and I soon got used to it. The first few months after my arrival were dull as far as the number of visitors. A quick check through the previous five years' guest books showed that only seven or eight hundred people visited each year.

Seldom having to give tours was a blessing at that time, for I was then able to devote hours learning about the wine business and Almadén in particular. I read books, books and more books and asked as many questions as possible. I hadn't come to the winery without any knowledge, though, because I still remembered what I had learned as a Pan Am stewardess. The Wine Advisory Board's course on wine appreciation was standard equipment for all Pan Am cabin personnel. We were expected to have some expertise on wines and liqueurs so as to reassure the monied passengers of those days that they were in cultured hands. (The fact that I never did know how to work the fire extinguisher I kept to myself.)

By early summer the visitors increased, we inaugurated private tasting parties, and by year's end, over 3,500 people had toured the winery. Through the years the numbers kept growing

29

until we became so saturated at 25,000 that we had to keep the tours down. Some wineries think nothing of having 100,000 or more people go through their facilities yearly, but Almadén was not terribly large, and, furthermore, there was no tasting room for the general public. Consequently, the majority of our visitors were primarily interested in learning how wine is made and more about the wine industry. We generally gave a souvenir, tax-paid, six-ounce bottle of Grenache Rosé to everyone over twenty-one. We had no retail sales room and there was no pressure, just the mutual fondness of learning about the world's most beneficial beverage.

Depending on the time I had and the importance of the visitors, I'd either bring them into the house for a little glass of sherry and a "break the ice" conversation before starting the tour or I'd start right in to save time. After an hour's tour we would sample wines and finish with a few snacks and a sip of champagne. Since we had domesticated quail and partridge on the grounds, the guests were usually overwhelmed when offered a freshly peeled, hard-boiled quail egg. Those little bobwhites are very prolific. Take it from me.

I was supposed to take VIPs to the tasting room built on the porch of the 1852 winery and special VIPs to the Main House for the butler to serve. The butler, though, objected to this extra work and to keep the peace I started bringing these people to my house. Home was never after the same.

On the average I would spend about two hours with the VIPs, the special people — either by reputation or because they were important in the wine or restaurant world — who came to Almadén.

Keeping my weight to one hundred pounds was no effort, what with greeting the first arrivals at 9:00 A.M. and waving *adeau* at 11:20, clearing the coffee table of empty bottles, used glasses, bowls, napkins and ashtrays, checking for messages and returning any urgent telephone calls, and then making a two-block dash to the office where the next-in-line had been kept waiting for me for about a half hour. I would bring them to my house and apologize for keeping them waiting and would cool their egos with a walk through the gardens praised by *Sunset* Magazine.

Then the tour, tasting and chatting. It's now 1:50 P.M. and the group is taking my directions to the nearest good restaurant for lunch. I'm eyeing the two occupants of a car parked in front of my cottage . . . they stare back. I find out they own three liquor stores in Ohio and were supposed to have come last week but didn't. I explain I'm still with other guests and could they wait? They will. How about a walk in the gardens? No, we'll wait in the car. A few minutes later the other guests are gone and I invite the couple into my cottage. As they sit down I whisk away the bottles, ashtrays and glasses from the previous group and am ready to entertain this new couple. The phone rings and I let it.

I need more than a couple of ounces of sherry. I also need to powder my nose. Both wait. We take fresh glasses and I fill theirs with champagne and mine with Perrier water from France. I explain. They smile and with glasses in hand we start the tour.

My 3:30 retailers are on time and I ask them to join the others. My patience is wearing a bit thin, but shortly the unexpected arrivals are on their way and I'm ready to hear from the newest group. They rave about the food in San Francisco and I hope they won't stop talking long enough to hear my stomach growl. They help me clear the coffee table of glasses, napkins, ashtrays and bottles and we decide to start the tour.

By 5:00 P.M. we're back at my house, foregoing the sampling but sipping champagne and cracking walnuts, pecans and Brazils. We find we have mutual friends, which makes the visit more interesting and relaxing for me. At 5:45 they say they should go; at 6:30 when they mention it again I don't change the subject. I wave them an affectionate farewell and return to the house to remove the emptied bottles, used napkins, dirty ashtrays . . . and my smile.

A check with the office message sheet shows a boyfriend with whom I had a tentative date had called three times but I don't feel like going out for a few drinks. I also don't feel like staying home for a few drinks. I don't even feel like having a bowl of soup and planning for the following day when two hundred fifty guests will be on the front lawn. I feel like sleep.

It took me a few months before I knew the names of the forty-eight people who then worked full time at the winery. I invariably went around with a notebook in my hand asking questions, writing down the answers, and learning more about wine. It has been a never-ending process.

I plied Al Huntsinger, the winemaster, with hundreds of questions. And I went after Armand Bussone, who was then the cellarmaster and is now Al's assistant winemaker, and he was just as patient with the naive girl who knew so little. Armand is from a wine making family; his father was the winemaker for Paul Masson when Masson was alive and he undoubtedly had to summon all his reserve to cope with this female newcomer. Both he and Al were wonderful to me, a scared young woman trying to make it in the man's world of wine.

The Benoists had a library full of books on wine and each day I tried to read for several hours. I read every one I could. About twenty percent were in French, German or Italian. I shall confess that of the more than one hundred books I read from their library, all but ten percent were boring and only four or five really held my interest. The percentages have remained the same even after ten years.

Some days I might have started off in a sour mood if the visitors had not turned downward lines into a smile of satisfaction. I enjoy people, and even if they aren't VIPs, they are individual human beings to me and I usually found something fascinating to remember.

I realized my job was secure when I had one of my earliest tours okayed by an international wine expert, none other than *the* Frank Schoonmaker.

I had been fast becoming an integral part of the flora and fauna of the place when I was called over to the Benoist house by Lisette, the sweet Belgian Cordon Bleu chef in residence at Almadén. "Mary, Mr. Benoist wants you to join him, and Mrs. Benoist and their guest, for cocktails and dinner."

When this request went out there was no escape, especially if you lived right across the courtyard. The boss was there and he expected you to be around if that was his wish. Luckily I understood this and I had been trained, again by newspapers, to be always available. Also, I was not married and I had a long-suffering mother.

I dressed quickly and fifteen minutes later was being ushered into the parlor by the butler.

Frank was the first American to spring upon the wine scene. As a student at Princeton in the 1920s he decided, while on summer vacation in Europe, to write a newspaper column about wine for a New York newspaper. In the 1930s he had a series of major articles in *The New Yorker*, which later expanded into his *The Complete Wine Book*. In that day there was no American writing on wine and Frank became one of the first accepted internationally by the European wine industry. He has been in the forefront of recognition ever since.

So, with this great man, I faced my future and gave a tour, my first to be acclaimed as worthwhile.

Was I scared? Silly question. But we had had some champagne for an hour before we began the tour and consequently my knees were not shaking. I knew I had been tutored by experts so I kept to the basics, added a few jokes of my own, and later Frank told Louie, "You've got yourself a good tour director and hostess. She knows what she's talking about."

I relaxed for the rest of the evening, but I remembered to thank Frank, and since then I've had the pleasure of meeting him many times. I felt if I could gain his acceptance, I could learn even more as the months went by.

To me, Frank looked like Dr. Kinsey. He had short, short hair clipped with tufts sticking up. He has the same barber today.

Stemming from his OSS days as a master spy, he has had one illness after another. Through these bouts and the passing years he has maintained a sweetness that invites outsiders to shed their masks of cautiousness. Once engaged in more than ten minutes of conversation, Frank is a goner; he's good for hours to help you solve whatever problems you have, or to tell you what he thinks of new wines.

The author of many books on wine and the owner of his own import firm, Frank has been a consultant for Almadén for thirty years while remaining the only non-French *membre diplômé* of the French Wine Academy.

I was flattered when called to join a select group of wine men for a professional wine tasting, one of whom was Frank, so I arrived at 9:00 A.M. in my feminine best, which included wearing a lovely perfume for the occasion. It was only my third professional wine tasting and I was still learning the ropes.

We were well into the first sampling when Al Huntsinger took me aside to say, much to my chagrin, "Mary, go bathe." I was shocked as he explained that my perfume was filling the tasting room's air so much that the men could not detect the bouquet of the wine.

I dissolved from the room, broke the shower-taking record and returned without a trace of perfume to find I had missed only two of the ten different wines listed for the day's tasting.

Al later told me that Frank had been hesitant about mentioning my perfume, but that he himself had put up with the scent several times before and decided it was time to give me the word, saving Frank the embarrassment.

Years later I told the producer of the *To Tell the Truth* television show about the incident and he decided to ask the "real" Frank Schoonmaker to be on the show.

Even experts can be fooled. Mike Bo, former winemaster for San Martin, once put one over on Frank and Ollie Goulet by selling them twenty thousand gallons of Zinfandel, which they thought was Cabernet Sauvignon. Frank and Ollie came to San Martin to buy some bulk wine (almost all wineries have to supplement their supply from other wineries). The three of them tasted a bit and Mike decided to amuse himself by passing some superb Zinfandel off as Cabernet. Now, a good Zinfandel, which has been aged for five or six years, starts to take on the characteristics of a Cabernet, but since both Frank and Ollie were two of the finest tasters in the country, Mike figured they should be able to tell the difference. This wine was about seven years old and since it came from Mike's hands, which meant from the hands of one of the country's top winemakers, it presented quite a challenge.

Mike avoided saying whether the wine was Zinfandel or Cabernet, but simply asked: "Now, what do you think of this gem?" They all sipped, sipped some more, and then compared it with some other wines. Both Frank and Ollie agreed that the batch they were studying was one of the finest of the Cabernets.

And so twenty thousand gallons of Zinfandel gloriously masquerading as Cabernet was sold to Almadén. The masters bought it and Mike got the laugh.

Frank may have missed on that one, but he never missed as far as I was concerned. I love the guy.

Almadén's tours were considered one of the three or four best in the country, and by many, the best. They conveyed tradition, color and informality. They contained no memorized speeches, just the personality of the guide, whether it was me, Louie Benoist, Al or one of my assistants, and the guest learned about wine at the same time.

The winery combined the old with the new. German visitors often exclaimed, "*Ach*, how clean!" as Mr. Benoist insisted the plant be kept spotless. In fact, we received a plaque from

General Foods and a letter saying they felt they could bake off our floors! Louie often toured the premises with a whistle that he would blow at his slightest displeasure, summoning a worried staff member. (Harkening back to his submarine days, the winery also had ships' bells and barometers. But, thank heavens, no gangplanks.)

Like most wineries, Almadén considered people who sell wine (distributors, liquor store managers, wholesalers, restaurant managers, owners of chain stores or bar owners) as VIPs, or, indirectly, those people who write columns on travel, wine or food. We also gave special treatment to influential people, doctors, lawyers, heads of companies or civic dignitaries.

Many more people came under the general heading of VIP, so many, in fact, that it was sometimes a difficult decision as to who made the list. We would have liked to treat everyone that way, but the pocketbook wouldn't take it.

Almadén and Beaulieu Vineyards in Napa County had a sometime (if unmentioned) "thing" going as to who could entertain the most illustrious of the nonlocal or foreign visitors. I'm sure that Almadén won hands down because we always seemed available. I was on the job.

From housewives (who I think should be the real VIPs because they do most of the buying) to doctors, lawyers, schoolteachers, schoolchildren, truck drivers, grocery clerks, secretaries, professional golfers, and actors, we ran the gamut of walk-in visitors. Often we had "name" drop-ins, presidents of large companies, heads of banks, presidents of universities. Since these people could be very helpful to our sales, my days were often fourteen-hour affairs fitting them all in.

When we knew in advance that special guests were coming, we allowed more time for them and I tried to fit a tour to their particular interests. There was a constant stream of winemakers, chemists, vineyard managers, general managers of wineries and others from throughout the wine world who beat a path to our door. Ray Beckwith and Christopher Hancock of Penfolds Wines of Australia were fascinating and understandable (some accents of the so-called English speaking peoples I simply can't catch). Freddy van Zyl of South Africa's Cooperative Wine Growers Association, Bernard Portet of Chateau Lafite-Rothschild, Gérard Toupet of the Meurice Group of hotels in Paris and many others presented me with the opportunity to learn still more about the international wine world, and were all helpful in answering my many questions.

Alexander Smith, the export manager of the famous Gonzalez Byass Company of Spain, taught me more about sherries in an hour than I'd learned from my many hours of studying the sherry cellars at Almadén. Alex was particularly interested in us since we had been taking a good part of the trade away from Spanish sherries and he had flown out from New York specifically for a visit.

After a short tour of the sherry cellars, he explained what to look for in fine sherries, as we sipped some of Almadén's, naturally. He inadvertently told me why I often get an asthma attack from sherry, particularly from those of Spain. In my case it's often because the yeast cells left in the bottle affect my allergies. I didn't let on that his famous "Tío Pepe," the most popular brand in the United States, guarantees me an asthma attack after just two ounces.

Sometimes even royalty came unexpectedly.

One afternoon as I was leaving the vineyard, two couples got out of a car parked in front of my cottage. The guests included the son and daughter of King Leon of the Wallis Islands. H.R.H. Asipau Mulikihaamea Matekitoga, the daughter of the King, was soft spoken, tall, with brown skin tones more like the upper-class society of Thailand, rather than the darker coloring of Polynesians we see in the travel brochures. Her "brother," Pai Pai Mulikihaamea Matekitoga (who was adopted by the King), his blond American wife and Andy White of San Jose's branch of American Savings and Loan had come so the Princess could see the workings of a California winery.

We had no trouble consuming Blanc de Blancs. After the VIP tour, many pictures were taken in the gardens as they extended their sincere invitations to me to visit the Princess and the King when I came to the Wallis Islands.

One obstacle I encountered when entertaining visitors in the tasting room in my cottage was the oak table and chairs. The table was square and two hundred years old, coming from a Franciscan monastery dining room when some of the missions were sacked by the Mexican government in the early 1800s. It had wooden pegs instead of nails and while the chairs were of a much later date, they had only three legs, representing the Trinity, to match the original set.

The cottage was so old that the floors were uneven from settling, particularly in the tasting room. When one first sat down in this slanted room it wasn't too bad, but after a few minutes almost everyone noticed a list. Usually they attributed it to too much drinking and it could be embarrassing when a visitor didn't want to try any more wine after having only a few ounces. It called for some fast talking when someone would lean over to emphasize a point and his chair would topple. I figured the best solution was to give them more champagne and let the room balance itself.

Most visitors were content to take the tour, see the grounds and receive the sample bottle of Grenache Rosé. They left thinking they had seen one of the best wineries in the United States, and they had. But some loud-mouths and assorted know-it-alls arrived too frequently to suit my taste. I had one standing rule: when someone gives trouble, either by their actions or insulting words, politely ask them to tone down or walk to the nearest exit and end the tour. The others could complete the tour later. I promised my guides I would back them up and I knew that Peter Jurgens would back me up. In all the years I was at Almadén, only six or seven obnoxious people had to be evicted, politely.

One unusual tour was given to a women's group of about thirty-five who were expected to be accorded a forty-five minute tour and a forty-five minute tasting before their bus drove them to a nearby restaurant for lunch. I noticed one member of this matronly group because she kept moving right under my chin whenever I would stop to chat about some particular feature of the winery. She was a stout, tightly corsetted fifty-eight, and had on an expensive tweed suit and a lovely small straw hat with a foot-long feather, heralding spring, no doubt. Everytime she came near me I felt like sneezing; she was forever nodding at my remarks and brushing my face or arms with that feather.

After awhile I noticed the feather — and the woman — were missing. Glancing around I found her on her hands and knees, mouth to the dripping spout of a wine barrel, her feather bobbing. It was quickly becoming wine soaked from the dribble, but she was doing fine. When I requested that she rejoin the tour, she remarked: "Okay, sweetie. But when are we going to drink?"

Sometimes our San Francisco office forgot to use the telephone and I found myself with an unexpected tour. One of the most enjoyable of them was one hundred members of the charity-minded men's organization, E. Clampus Vitus. They brought their own band, which played constantly, and provided a *tour de farce*, and fun, even though I squirmed a bit as they carried me about on their shoulders.

And certainly one of the most shocking tours I gave was to a group of eight from England, four of them with titles. A little after 10:00 P.M. my phone jingled and I awoke to the sound of the Benoist's Polish butler telling me I was needed for a special tour. "Am I really needed?" His cool reply, "Yes."

The guests had arrived on the spur of the moment about 7:00 P.M., had a few drinks and a light meal, and then decided they really wanted to see the winery. With glass in hand we headed there. I had the keys (which also entitled me to open up every time a false alarm sent the firemen — usually between one and five in the morning) and quickly decided this was to be a fast tour.

One of the couples was recently married and the wife had just previously divorced one of the *crème de la crème* of the British nobility. They were far less interested in a wine tour than in consummating their new union.

Midway through I sensed that only two or three people cared what was going on, but in order not to hurt the host's feelings I continued. I was a veteran by then and used to people, so I seldom waxed impatient, impolite or perplexed. But this time I was nonplussed.

At the next-to-last room I was giving a three-minute windup talk when I noticed the newlyweds were missing. I had turned off the lights in each room as we left and I began getting a little nervous. When they didn't appear as we entered the last room, I asked the others to wait for a moment while I went back to look.

There they were, against one of the twenty-five-thousand-gallon redwood tanks in a darkened room, the noble husband making love to the female member of the aristocracy.

I instinctively said, "Oh, pardon me." I was shocked. They were not.

We all went back to the Benoists. I immediately went home.

CHAPTER IV

VIPs ON TOUR

Whether used for entertaining or as get-away-from-it-all abodes, Kay and Louie Benoist maintained five homes in California.

There was their Nob Hill apartment in San Francisco, the Palm Springs villa that had been in the Benoist family for eons, and the very private cottage in Aptos. (Said "cottage" was five bedrooms and three baths plus private beachfront with the landscaping done by Thomas Church, the *ne plus ultra* landscape architect. I well remember Kay's unhappiness when told by Tommy that it might take him some time to design an aviary for their bird collection as he was working on Cabrillo College in Santa Cruz.)

To me, the most important homes for entertaining were the Almadén, Los Gatos, residence, complete with live-in servants and, of course, the Paicines vineyard's main house which was one hundred years old and was formerly part of the famed Sykes ranch. It was to the superbly staffed house in Paicines that the Benoists went most of their weekends. Prior to the death of Ollie, they spent more time at Almadén, but by the early 1960s, Paicines had become their main retreat. Since both Kay and Louis Benoist have exceptionally good taste in everything, the houses were showplaces.

And, whenever the Benoists were in residence at either

estate, there was some kind of a party going on. I was kept busy helping to entertain celebrities of various worlds: business, art, theatre, opera, political, on one side of the courtyard at Almadén; on the other side, at the winery and my home, I talked with VIPs of the wine and liquor industry.

But VIPs, whether boring, clever, or just a famous name to give special attention to, come in all races, figures and personalities and deserved my attention. I had been on the job only a few days when I met my first, Barbara Hutton, then between husbands but soon to marry her seventh, and third prince, a Vietnamese.

I had never seen her in person and was surprised to find she was so frail looking. Although of medium height, she weighed perhaps ninety-five pounds and was constantly hovered over by an entourage of friends, fickle or honest I couldn't tell. I know I liked her even though I did little more than add a bit of extra conversation to the afternoon.

The first VIP to visit us that I really wanted to meet was Alec Waugh, the British novelist, who was then riding a wave of popularity in the literary world. It was a dinner for eight and from the initial handshake and "how do you do" I was a fan of Mr. A. Waugh.

We chatted, I flirted, sipped champagne and nibbled on pâté and crackers. I asked him questions concerning his books and his more famous brother, Evelyn, and how he felt about the movie made from his novel, *Island in the Sun.*

Speaking frankly he told me that he was so thrilled to finally make it big in America by having his book made into a movie, that he kept walking by theaters where the film was playing so often he began to fear people might think he was picketing!

He delighted me with his humanness when I asked him about his book, *In Praise of Wine.* His sincerity was immediate. "Frankly, I can't recall. I'd have to go back to the book for reference. Once I'm finished with something, I forget so much of it as I get involved in another subject."

After some champagne, I dared to tell him about the rude episode I'd suffered through because of his brother, Evelyn. Alec was all ears.

Retrogressing to my college days at Ursuline in New Orleans, I recalled how I had written Evelyn Waugh for an interview for the school's quarterly literary magazine. I enclosed a list of questions that I felt were neither too personal nor mundane and waited. One month went by, then two and finally three with no answer.

Then came a call from the dean's office where a livid Mother Superior showed me a letter from The Man. In prose that had sold millions of books and made him the toast of the literary world for thirty years, Mr. E.W. raged about "some illiterate orphan from your asylum" having requested an interview and asking *the* most personal of questions. Furthermore, he said, I was so stupid that I'd enclosed U.S. postage stamps for return mail! He said he knew the Ursulines had come to the New World to teach the Indians and other savages, but that he thought the nuns were wise enough not to let them get out of hand.

Mother Superior was not fazed by the fact that the stamps had been enclosed by someone in the dean's office and that I did not get my interview. But the fact that her religious order had been reduced to the intellectual level of teaching "savages" was the ultimate end. Waugh's books were to be banned from the library and his letter torn to bits.

Sanity prevailed after a few hours. Mother Superior gave no order regarding the books and included the letter, at my suggestion, into the archives with other fascinating material dating from the school's founding in 1727.

Alec believed every word of it and noted the consistency of his brother's eccentric actions. He listened intently when I told him it had appeared in print that his brother had been appearing in public in recent years with an ear trumpet two feet long!

I by no means found Alec Waugh a stuffy Englishman. But I did find the handwriting on his personal calling card so tiny that he could have made some side money by writing the Lord's Prayer on the coins you can buy at some fairs. I also wished I'd been able to talk with him even further into the night.

Every few years the Romanov name resurfaces to headlines. Recently it was because of the movie *Nicholas and Alexandra* and a few years before that it was because of a suit brought by a woman calling herself the Grand Duchess Anastasia.

Prior to my vineyard days I had met a Romanov myself, Hollywood restaurateur Mike Romanoff, who was just as fabled as all the others.

But the Romanovs who visited the Benoists were the real thing. Prince Vasili is the nephew of the last Czar of Russia but, unless he were to appear in regal robes and crown, no one would ever know. Vasili, as he prefers to be called, is about as unpretentious as any democratic person ever could be. When we first met he was chatting with the gardener about getting fresh leeks. It wasn't until later, when I did a double take, that I realized the soft-spoken man who had introduced himself as Vasili Romanov in the garden was leading a group I was to join that afternoon for luncheon.

Natasha, his wife, usually arrived with a pair of white dogs (not Borzois) and spoke with such a lovely voice that I was almost mesmerized as each vowel and consonant came off in deep, velvety sounds.

Since they were frequent visitors to Almadén, I saw them often and once was able to engage the prince in conversation about Russia when he was a boy. I felt sorry for them, refugees from their homeland, as he told me of his flight. I marveled at his almost fatalistic acceptance of life's low blow — having had so very much and losing it all.

One further note. Hanging inside the porch of the Main House at Almadén is an old-fashioned, tin mailbox painted black. Stuck on it is a label with a crest boldly declaring Romanov Vodka. The prince, it seems, needed some money and sold the rights to the name to an American distiller. He gave the mailbox to the Benoists as a gift and one evening playfully slapped the liquor sticker on it.

I'm sure that National Distillers, now the owners of Almadén, have no idea how the sign got there, if they've even noticed it. But the little box hangs as a bit of memorabilia of the Romanovs and, consequently, a tidbit of history.

As can be seen, the Benoist guest list comprised more than a sprinkling of international society. When I was to tour them I was usually given advance notice by the San Francisco office, but much too often people arrived expecting special treatment without my knowing they were due. (In all fairness, sometimes they just dropped in.) To say we went above and beyond the call of duty again and again is no exaggeration. Most of the time we extended ourselves and it paid off handsomely for the company. But the beauty of the operation was that — to a person — everyone involved enjoyed what he was doing.

Now and then a group of socialites would arrive whom the Benoists were unable to attend to. Then, sometimes Mrs. Elinor Chatfield-Taylor would serve as hostess and I would assist her.

I always remember Elinor in a stunning lime green summer picture hat and a print cotton dress dispensing charm to a group of Latin Americans who were, I'm sure, ready to sweep her off her feet, wrap her in their best linen and take her back to their homes. She is lovely, quite personable and, best of all to me, a woman who cares about other women. She never appeared jealous if all the men weren't paying attention to her at once; she was willing to share the wealth. I like that and I've always liked Elinor.

She had scads of friends who are society with a capital S, if there still is such a thing, but until I left Almadén I never knew that the hyphenated Chatfield-Taylor (Robert), her ex-husband, had married the deb of all times, Brenda Frazier, in 1957. They are still married and Elinor, entirely without malice, entertains her ex-husband's friends, even being her charming self when entertaining for Victoria Kelly, Brenda Frazier's daughter from her previous marriage to "Shipwreck" Kelly, a way-back-when Kentucky football hero.

One woman, often mentioned in society columns throughout the world, whom I found particularly interesting was Elgie Catherwood, whose husband, Cummins Catherwood, has endowed foundation after foundation in the family name.

I first met her in 1963 when she visited with her son, David Coates, for lunch. I found her pleasant, but after an hour she suddenly blossomed. The secret was that she was no longer with a stranger and I was able to see more than a sophisticated, smart woman; I saw a fascinating, vivacious lady.

Elgie has, to my thinking, some of the most gorgeous jewels I have ever seen. Being from New Orleans, and having been brought up with people much older than I, I was used to a lot of gingerbread diamonds, emeralds and rubies on dowagers, like those seen in pictures of the late Mrs. John Jacob Astor or the late Mrs. Cornelius Vanderbilt. I've always hated such gems, including tiaras, when they were worn for anything less than a state occasion. I think the Italians are magnificent with gems. They are able to work in many of them without making them look like pre-1955 fake jewelry or a Hawaiian sport shirt motif.

So I appreciated and admired Elgie's jewelry. In fact, if I were the jealous type I would have shown green. Unfortunately, time and money have prevented me from seeing her more often, but an occasional visit at Almadén and postcards or notes, as well as many newspaper items, have kept me in touch with her life.

One afternoon I was called over to the Main House to help entertain a group that included Anita Loos, a woman whose mind I admire. Both she and Cecil Beaton were currently working on the movie *My Fair Lady*. (I later saw the movie and noticed that Gordon Bau was credited as head makeup man. He had made me up for a screen test in the 1950s, but when I found out RKO was thinking of me as a foil for some cowboy in a series, I had no trouble forgetting the test. Horses are beautiful animals. I love to see them in action, but they also bring hay fever and they have big teeth — the better to bite you with, my dear.)

Anita Loos was fascinating. I remembered a worldly nun telling me that if I wanted to know about *life*, be sure to read Anita Loos. So, I expected to learn a lot from her, but how can you ask your first one hundred questions about men when you have only fifteen minutes to really talk?

She was so small I felt Bunyanesque. She still wore her hair pixie short with bangs. So did I then. But she was about four feet ten whereas I was an enormous five feet, and she looked about ninety pounds while I was one hundred. There wasn't that much difference but I thought her Lilliputian.

The biggest shock, however, came when the bouyant Anita, the author of the ever popular *Gentlemen Prefer Blondes*, told me: "I hardly ever drink wine. But I would like to know something about it; do tell me." I was so disappointed to learn that the creator of that all-girl flirt, Lorelei Lee, lacked the familiarity of toying with the stem of a wineglass.

Also at that party were Michael Taylor and socialite Whitney Warren. Michael, a nationally known interior decorator, had helped Kay Benoist very much with the Almadén residences at Los Gatos and Paicines as well as with their staysail schooner, *Le Voyageur*.

Before buying *Le Voyageur*, the Benoists owned a ninety-eight-foot ketch, the *Morning Star*, which they sold to the late Clay Callaway, who was quite a sailor and onetime husband to Pia Lindstrom. I recall sharing moments of anxiety with Louie and Kay when Clay ran aground on a coral reef while in a trans-Pacific race. Luckily he was a good enough sailor to save himself and the ship.

If the *Morning Star* was a cruising ship *par excellence*, *Le*

Voyageur was in a super class by herself. Springs, mattresses, new sails and every item that could be monogrammed was. Complete china was from Abercrombie and Fitch, the sheets, pillow slips and fluffy white towels all carried the monogram — Mr. B's flag crossed with that of the St. Lawrence Rowing Club. The Benoists treated the yacht like a grand lady. They installed a floating wine cellar and saw to it that the bathrooms (much too elegant to be called heads) had either full-size showers or tubs.

Michael was a guest on several of the short voyages (the Benoists never took long trips anyplace in the world). He recounted Benoist's showing Charlie Chaplin movies on the sails. Now, Michael's been around quite a bit, but even he was moved by eating caviar, drinking champagne and watching Chaplin on the sails of a hundred-fourteen-foot ship cruising off the coast of Mexico.

(In the spring of 1968, Louie Benoist donated *Le Voyageur* to the U.S. Navy, and in a formal ceremony at Annapolis, it became the flagship of the Naval Academy. Hovering over the ship, no doubt, was the shade of Louie's great-great-great-grandfather, Benjamin Stoddert, who witnessed the U.S. Navy grow from three frigates when he was Secretary of the Navy under President John Adams to more than fifty ships.)

Anita was fun and easy to please, because everything pleased her. She looked a well-preserved, vital sixty. In a seersucker suit and spectator pumps, with her short hair and bangs as a trademark, we posed for pictures. I wanted an eight-by-ten to frame but to my annoyance the photographer was so far away that you could see us only with the aid of a magnifying glass.

More than those of movie or TV stars, who seldom seem interested in wine, the boys and girls around the winery wanted the autographs of royalty, so I always tried to tip them off when some were due. Consequently, when the Duke and Duchess of Gloucester visited, all hands had scraps of paper for them to sign. The Duke is the younger brother of the late Duke of Windsor and an uncle to Queen Elizabeth. He looks like one pictures a duke, like a grouse hunter in baggy tweeds with plus fours and a couple of feathers in his hat. A change of his outfit to canvas or duck and he would be ready for a safari in the late '20s or early '30s.

We were quite disappointed when their son, Prince William, was unable to visit. We had been expecting him the entire time he had been studying at Stanford, but something always came up. However, the Benoists did entertain him in San Francisco.

The Duke was hard of hearing — even my loud voice.

The Duchess was gentle and also tweedy — someone used to throwing out the first spade of dirt at this or that hospital dedication — and was particularly interested in the salaries the workers made. Most foreigners were usually eager to learn such statistics because the workers here earned so much compared with their countrymen, a fact that was at times discomforting.

It wasn't until months later that I found I had made a faux pas by putting my hand on the Duchess' shoulder to guide her through a passageway during the tour. Apparently touching the royal family is a no-no, but she was too polite and poised to reprimand me, and I didn't lose any sleep when I learned of my indiscretion.

When Peter Townsend came to the vineyard, he was still very much in the limelight although his romance with Princess Margaret had ended three or four years earlier and he was married to a young French girl. He was small in stature, about five-foot-five, and was in the U.S. (representing his father-in-law's vineyards) to check out the reasons why French wines were losing so many sales to American wines.

He was affable, although not much of a talker, and was quite nervous about the expected arrival of a new child. He phoned his wife to get the latest status report and showed a deep affection for her. Both the Belgian chef, Lisette, and I felt just as romantic over his concern and believed that even though he didn't marry a princess, love had conquered all. The baby, a boy, was born three days later while Townsend was in New York.

A society writer could easily fill her column day after day by just taking notes of the visitors Almadén received, from the Christian de Guignes, the Ralph Davies, Audrey Hepburn's mother, the Baroness Ella van Heemstra, the J.D. Zellerbachs, Samuel F.B. Morses to Prentis Cobb Hale, who recently hit the headlines when he married Denise Minnelli. It was a kaleidescope.

One restaurant owner furnished amusement whenever he came for lunch. Since making a hit on Broadway in *Zorba the Greek*, Louis Gundunas and his wife, Peggy, no longer found time for lengthy visits, but before that he would dance and — when the spirit moved him — pick up a loaded table by his teeth while Sonja Norayan, his featured dancer, sinuously slithered about . . . all for the fun of it.

Most of the time entertaining was more work than fun. With some people you had nothing in common, except the fact that both of you were holding a wine glass, and sometimes a biggie arrived carrying a chip on his shoulder about your wines that brought out diplomacy in full force as you answered, with absolute honesty, all of his questions.

Al Huntsinger and Armand Bussone were a marvelous help. Whenever they sensed that I was not being believed, they would "take the ball" and launch into such a detailed account that even the most skeptical of visitors had to remove the shield from his eyes and the plugs from his ears.

Day's end sometimes found me so drained of energy, mentally and physically, that even another glass of cold champagne couldn't revive a worn-out girl who had been determined to make a believer out of a skeptic. But I thoroughly enjoyed entertaining people, particularly other wine people, explaining the history of Almadén and telling of its hopes for the future.

The California Wine Institute and the Wine Advisory Board sent their new employees down to be shown around, as they did with special visitors from out of state or country. Working with the former president of the Institute, Don McColly, was a pleasure and working with the manager of the Advisory Board, Dan Turrentine, has never been work at all, he's so willing to help. I loved to see Don Bonhaus, former field manager of the Advisory Board, who often came with newly hired men to hear me spread the Gospel about California wines, and who dubbed me "California's First Lady of Premium Wines." The label has stuck so much that I still receive mail with that subtitle.

There is an absolute doll working for the Wine Institute named Doris Paulsen. She's been with them for some thirty years, although she must have started at age five because she's so young looking. Everyone in the industry relies upon her and if I wore all the hats Doris does, I'd take them all off to her.

I always got a special lift out of instructing airline personnel because I'd once been a Pan Am stewardess. I figured I knew what they needed to know and what would be superfluous. TWA, United, Continental, Western and Pan American's stewardesses and their bosses were greeted by our hospitality. Many Pan Am executives periodically visited the winery and I had fun catching up on the latest doings of special friends, including Roger Wolin, and Jack Thale, who had once been an ace Chicago *Daily News* foreign correspondent.

There were many newsmen and women who visited Almadén, not always in quest of stories, either. A dear friend, Jeanne Bellamy of the Miami *Herald*, and active in the Audubon Society, had been attending one of its meetings in the Northwest and stopped over for a brief visit with me. In the midst of gossip, she told me the story of a former Audubon member and newsman who is known for chasing skirts, which he does without subtlety. He was finally given his comeuppance by a young girl who slugged him when he mistook her for a rosey-breasted tit willow.

I was lucky. There were seldom any visitors whose company I couldn't take. And there were many whose company I could have enjoyed for hours more. The conversation was usually about wine, but it often drifted into other fields, and I could always learn something new.

In fact, I was once all agog while showing Mortimer Caplan, then head of the U.S. Internal Revenue Service, around the winery. After about forty-five minutes I asked the one question I wanted to know: "Mr. Caplan, can you tell me the easiest way to make out my 1040?"

His answer startled and delighted me. "Miss Lester," he said straightforwardly, "I don't know how to fill out a Form 1040. I never have been able to figure it out. And, furthermore, I'm resigning very shortly to return to private law practice."

I hurriedly passed this last bit of info on to the San Jose *News* as a scoop.

I also resolved to continue using a reliable tax consultant to handle my forms.

CHAPTER V

DINNERS, LUNCHEONS AND BARBEQUES

What with taxes, the high cost of living and the other entrapments of modern life, it may be a little difficult to envision a couple with five homes, two planes, a large yacht and some of the country's best champagne to drink. The Louis Benoists had it all. You might say I was their resident entertainer. Fortunately, rationality prevailed; I was only expected to help at their two vineyard residences, Almadén at Los Gatos and at Paicines which was near Monterey.

Except for those which are purely commercial, bulk operations, all wineries give special treatment to visitors who can help sell or promote the wines carrying their label. Some wineries give lovely luncheons or private dinners, besides allowing the general public to reserve the winery property for parties, for which a fee is usually charged.

Thanks to the many newspaper and magazine articles written about her over the years, extolling the delights of dining there, Almadén was the biggest freeload in the nation — although by no means were all of our guests freeloaders. But the publicity about how "in" it was to have lunch — and for those rare few, dinner — created a temptation too great for many who would otherwise be immune, in fact, immune to anything but tasting martinis.

49

We took groups to lunch, we gave special luncheons, we had barbeques and we had dinners. The dinners were seldom, meaning we gave only two or three a month because the servants objected, and if you can't keep the servants you lose more than just the dinners.

The groups entertained at lunch represented a variety of Americans from across the nation. At one time or another the Pennsylvania Liquor Control Board, the Wine and Food Society of Hollywood, members of the Scientific American, members of the European Wine Growers Association, and Navy officers and their wives from Treasure Island sat down at our table.

We entertained Harry Waugh of Bristol and London, Prince Louis de Polignac, the Duchess of Westminster, a dozen South African viticulturists. Members of the Gourmet Section of the Federated Women's Club of Los Altos were our guests as were a couple of dozen members of the Northern California Hotel and Motel Association and a group of geologists from the California State Division of Mines and Geology. (One of Almadén's wineries is exactly on the San Andreas Fault and sometimes there were more geologists around to measure the widening of the crevices than there were winemakers to measure sugar-acid ratios. I guess they began to like the place and decided to find out if it was worth worrying about all those oak casks splitting open. We were glad they worried and glad to have them.)

We gave luncheons for Almadén's sales personnel representing the fifty U.S. states and two or three times a month entertained growers from around the world. I became so used to cigar-smoking women that I had to laugh when I saw an American woman trying to enjoy a *ceegar*. She just didn't look like she had mastered how to hold it and I began to get uncomfortable as she puffed away. But even worse, my esthetic values were bruised whenever I saw an American male kiss a woman's hand. Few of them have the "feel" for it; they ought to stick to handshakes.

We became rapidly, gratefully and affectionately known to the U.S. State Department as a "winner": one of Uncle Sam's friends who was willing to entertain his special guests, capable of sending them on their way with the feeling they had been treated warmly and graciously, like visiting royalty. I keep telling myself that if I should ever decide to "defect" to Latin America, I've entertained so many of their bigwigs that I should surely be given sanctuary!

One luncheon that lasted into the late evening was given for the captain and officers of the USS *Benjamin Stoddert* (DDG-22). (This ship made the headlines in June, 1972, when one of her guns blew up on board the vessel, off the coast of Vietnam, killing two seamen.) She was named after the first Secretary of the U.S. Navy and was special to Mr. B because Stoddert was his great-great-great-grandfather. So Mrs. B went to Seattle to help christen her and eventually some of the crew came to the winery to be entertained. The boss's secretary, Marian Pieren, helped lend a pretty face and with her red hair, freckles and winsome way, was an instant success. Twenty-three naval officers and two young women translate into a glorious time — especially for the women.

The only thing that saved the men from being adulated was the fact that most of them were under thirty. Both Marian and I preferred older men so we loved having these young men cut in on us while dancing in the bistro of the Main House, but we were only flirting, which gave us time to concentrate on the essentials of the party. When the cars came around to pick up the men after lunch, Commander Walter Mcginniss, the ship's captain, asked us to be his guests for dinner that evening with the entire crew. It was an exciting evening . . . dulled only by the sixty-five mile drive back to Almadén alone.

When the State Department asked if we would entertain some visiting Masai tribesmen, I could hardly wait. Just as foreigners, and even some Americans, expect Indians to appear in leather, paint and feathers, I expected the Masai to appear in semi-native attire. After all, I've met more than one Scot who wears a kilt when not on parade. But these lovely gentlemen wore Bond Street clothing, spoke English with an upper-class accent, and hadn't appeared in their ceremonial clothing since childhood. They were all sons of chieftains and expressed surprise, and pleasure, that I had somewhat of a working knowledge of African affairs. (I always knew a subscription to *Intelligence Digest* would be valuable.)

After one of our national elections, four Members of Parliament from England who were touring parts of the U.S. stopped by for lunch and to see how wines — other than sherries — were made. Two of them were conservatives and the other two rather liberal. Listening to them cut each other up, always with an intellectual sarcasm laced with politeness, gentility and the touch of centuries of English civilization, was the high point of their visit. Maybe I learned more — or at least had more fun — than they did.

I correspond with one of them, the Honorable William W. Hamilton, M.P., the representative for West Fife, Scotland, so I enjoy reading newspaper and magazine accounts of his latest blasts at the British government. When Princess Margaret and Lord Snowden made a trip to the U.S., headlines heralded Bill's remarks in Parliament about the British government footing the bill for royalty's unofficial trips around the world. He's still among the leaders giving thumbs down on having the Queen's household expenses upped.

Not long ago, *Time* Magazine wrote how, in a letter to the London *Times*, "Scottish Laborite MP William Winter Hamilton publicly and unreservedly withdrew his House of Commons remark about Prince Charles being a 'young twerp.' " So, Bill's still going strong, amusing the public . . . and winning votes.

I'm aware that most people like souvenirs, so I tried to see that out-of-country (as well as out-of-state) VIPs were given a bottle of tax-paid wine, and if they desired, a set of wine bottle labels. Almadén's labels are the most unusual in the world; they contain not only the comments of one of the greatest internationally known wine authorities, Frank Schoonmaker, but the drawings of the famous French artist, Fabrés.

Missing a crested paper cocktail napkin or even a linen towel from one of the guest bathrooms, or a crested champagne glass (that was the least expensive of the crystal), didn't faze me as much as it did the butler, who regularly got into a tizzy.

But missing a twenty-five dollar Baccarat glass or a pair of solid silver Georgian salt shakers was another matter. Occasionally a member or two of a group would try lifting whatever could be carried out.

I remember one embarrassing scene when a retired rear admiral tried walking out with a salt shaker set. The butler had missed it while cleaning the table and lay in wait for the culprit. His microscopic eyes spied the sag in the admiral's jacket and he was never again piped aboard the Benoists' ship.

I was furious at one chamber of commerce group I had helped arrange a grandiose afternoon for. Their booty: one porcelain vase, one silver candelabra, two silver shakers, four silver pepper pots, eight silver wine tasting spoons (the kind found on a chain around a wine steward's neck) that were heirlooms, and a velvet cushion. When the butler presented me with the list of what was gone, I rivalled him in temper. After all, the chief of police had even been present!

I contacted the man in blue and, after profuse apologies, he assured me that everything would be returned. Early the next morning, while letting the cat in, the butler found two large paper sacks on the back porch containing everything but the velvet cushion. (Apparently the chief hadn't got to the seat of the matter.)

Psychiatrists pilfered the most. (Psychologists, on the other hand, were completely different.) It was the psychiatrists who were difficult to handle and the ones I hosted were — for the most part — completely out of it. I was fortunate if there were two or three out of a party of sixty with whom I could converse longer than five minutes. The only person who seems to think like a psychiatrist is another psychiatrist, which is explanation enough for me why their suicide rate is the highest of any profession.

I dreaded their arrival and looked forward to their departure. Their parties were always a "happening" all right, it's just that you wished most of it wouldn't happen.

My groups seemed to have enough foundation in Spanish to firmly believe in the *mi casa es su casa* adage. At one particular party they lost no time in making themselves at home, some partially disrobing, and going about fun and games; this included two couples who were relaxed enough to begin copulation, one behind the hedge by my back door and the other on the lawn in the pseudoprivacy of a sun umbrella. Meanwhile, their companions went on drinking and laughing and I went looking for a tranquilizer. They could have gone on for days, but I was determined to put my size six double A foot down and call a halt to the bacchanalian bash before the normal quitting time for the afternoon.

I did, and with the burly presence of some of the help, the group left. And with them went assorted pieces of silverware, some handmade and hand painted French crockery, Irish linen napkins and Irish linen tablecloths. They also took several bottles of uncorked champagne, a number of partially emptied bottles of wine and, naturally, the glasses to drink it from — by the dozen.

If I hadn't known better I would have consulted a psychiatrist to couch me out of my murderous mean, but the help and I relaxed with one of the cold bottles of champagne we still had left and I assured everyone the group would never return. The next day a letter was posted to our San Francisco office outlining my *general* objections and ending with a cursory, "If they come back, I go."

The janitor discovered some of the group's cache in the parking lot later, where their picnic had evidently continued.

No matter what the meal at Almadén, the food was of the finest and the service impeccable. While yachting, the Benoists' meals were generally simpler and lighter, although some could be ornate. But it was dinners for eight or twelve — or for large affairs of fifty or sixty guests — that turned into banquets talked about for months.

Such was a two-day feast billed as a meeting of the Confrerie des Chevaliers du Tastevin. Numbering fifty-four, the partying started at the Paicines vineyards on Saturday evening and ended Sunday afternoon at the Los Gatos vineyards.

I remember the Benoists anxiously waiting for society photographer-columnist Jerome Zerbe to jet from New York. He was bringing in for them the first course of fresh Iranian Beluga caviar.

There were five courses in all. The caviar, along with Blanc de Blancs champagne, was served on the terrace before the party moved to tables surrounding the lighted pool for dinner. Small candles were centered on the tables and an almost full moon added its benefits to a lovely summer evening. First the guests had crayfish, followed by quail with *foie gras*, a beef fillet with Bearnaise sauce, salad and cheese. And, of course, accompanying wines.

Clifford Weihman, the Grand Pilier General, who had flown in from New York for the dinner, told me it was one of the finest Chevaliers' meetings he had ever attended. Mr. Weihman has one of the greatest private wine cellars in the world and it is my regret that I had no time for a lengthy chat with him and a favorite wine and food connoisseur of mine who flew in from Beverly Hills, handsome Hernando Courtright. As founder of the San Francisco branch of the Chevaliers, Mr. Courtright hosts an elegant white-tie dinner for the Northern and Southern California group each year at his hotel, the Beverly Wilshire.

The next day the group assembled for a tour of the winery, after they had sipped champagne and eaten peeled hard-boiled partridge eggs, and thin slices of toast with even thinner slices of ham cured at the Benoist Virginia home and flown in for the day.

Then came lunch under the trees on the side of the lawn. To prevent the trees from adding any of their own flavoring to the menu, outsized silk-lined white umbrellas sheltered the guests. The meal included partridge with truffles, shrimp with lobster, braised celery, fresh strawberries seeped in cognac, champagne and Cointreau, and plates of freshly baked macaroons.

It wasn't a weekend for diets.

Quite often the Benoists' flag was raised to show they were in residence for a few days and I was frequently invited to dine with them. I have found that people who not only have a great deal of money, but are accustomed to wealth (and there is a big difference), at times eat sparingly. I guess they have to or they would weigh more than the late Aga Khan. When we dined together, the meal would usually consist of a light soup, lamb chops or fillet of beef, and a salad with cheese. The Benoists followed the European custom of eating their salad last, a final, light tribute to the meal.

Their formal dinners were for anywhere from eight to twenty-eight people, although they preferred no more than twelve so as to have easy conversation.

A Beauveau tapestry hung at one end of the dining room, with a small solarium at the other filled with ferns and additional greenery. A fireplace on one side provided warmth (and woe to anyone who sat too near on a not-too-cold night — one's fanny dreamed easily of wanderlust), while beeswax candles were the only other illumination . . . at a cost of forty dollars an evening.

Often I was called over to the Main House (a name I chose rather than the Ranch House, which Kay abhorred) on an hour's notice. And sometimes on a few days' notice. At times the Benoists just wanted to talk with someone else and at other times they thought I could add brightness to a group, especially when it was a threesome, they and a male.

Once dinner for the three of us was interrupted by a telephone call for Louie from movie actor Michael Wilding, who was both agent to and ex-husband of Elizabeth Taylor. He wanted to know if he could rent *Le Voyageur*, the Benoists' yacht, on behalf of Elizabeth and her husband, Richard Burton. They had lived aboard her while filming "Cleopatra," in the days when they were first together, long before Elizabeth became one of the world's most beautiful grandmothers. It was an interesting conversation, but Mr. B was unwilling to rent, lease or sell. He thought Elizabeth gorgeous and was all congratulations to Burton, but would not part with his ship.

Mr. B always displayed Southern gallantry. He'd walk me across the courtyard to my door after dinner and give a courtly bow as he bid me goodnight, he called me "Miss Mary" except in strictly business conversation, and he had a formal respect for my femininity; but he could be impish as well. More than once I detected horns beginning to sprout, but he was so charming that one would have to be a prude or thin-skinned to take offense at his devilish remarks.

One dinner party gave me an inkling of his humor. He and Kay were showing three of the male guests the famous mahogany-framed copper tub where Ziegfeld beauty Anna Held took that legendary bath in champagne, when one of the men suggested it be recreated for the benefit of the press.

Mr. B popped up with: "And I think Miss Mary here would be a fine replica." To my startled look, he wryly remarked, "Don't worry, you can wear a hair ribbon." With that, Mrs. B cried: "Auguste!" always the signal of a reprimand (Mr. B's middle name). The matter ended.

I still have the handwritten, embossed menu of a Christmas Eve dinner party for eight, held for the Duke and Duchess of Manchester, to recall an evening of scintillating conversation, superb food and drink.

The Duke, now married to the former Mrs. W.W. Crocker, widow of the San Francisco banker, was then married to his late wife, Nell.

The Duke immediately insisted that I call him "Mandy" and joined his wife in telling me stories about the Mau Mau in Kenya. I learned more in that conversation than I did reading Robert Ruark's book on the uprising. Mandy has a large estate in Kenya but most of the priceless heirlooms and other valuables have been shipped out of Africa, just in case.

Both the Manchesters were quite down-to-earth people. As far as that goes, I'll have to include their dog, Pernod, a tiny, white pooch who perpetually shivered and ignored the newspapers I had conveniently placed on the floor in the guest bathroom in favor of a fluffy white shag rug.

After the Christmas Eve meal, the Duchess confessed that she was about ready to spear the man on her right with her fork when the butler removed the utensils. The fellow had been running his hand up and down her leg, and then began wrapping his leg around hers, but the Duchess was saved from subsequent foreplay when he left, to go sing in the church choir!

Before dinner we often had caviar or escargot. The first course might be eggs aspic, each egg decorated with a miniature bunch of grapes made of black truffles with a tiny real grape leaf and tendril, and cucumbers in cream. The main dish could be partridge raised on the vineyard, with tiny potatoes and homegrown peas. A green salad and cheese followed, and then dessert, quite often my favorite, Crepes au Citron. Once again, wine came with each course.

Sometimes the Benoists followed the English habit of the men staying at the table for coffee and liqueurs while the women went into the parlor, and sometimes they did not. Although we eventually ended up in the same room, I was always happiest when the English kept their traditions to themselves.

Except in the worst of weather, which allowed us about eight months of the year free, we gave barbeques every weekend, and sometimes once or twice during the week as well. I gladly volunteered the use of my backyard when we first thought of having these affairs, to be open to the public by reservation only, because I thought we might have a dozen or so a year. Alas for the lawn! It was left with only December through March to regenerate its blades.

We hosted such groups as the International Order of Military Wine Tasters, the San Francisco Curling Club, the University of California Professors of Business Administration School, the Los Gatos Women's Federated Club, the Santa Clara County School Psychologists, the Connecticut General Life Insurance Company, the Palo Alto Junior Chamber of Commerce, the Duffers Golf Club of the Southern Peninsula, the East Bay Baldwin Organ Club, the Northern California Professional Photographers Association, the Food Machinery Corporation, not to mention Welcome Wagons, alumni groups and junior leagues. I hosted most of them. (Let me confess, it's not that I'm so heroic, it's just that if I didn't I had to leave for the day because the din kept me from getting anything done, anyway.)

I had a permanent staff of three plus a chef, and several other reliable people to help when the crowds reached the seventy to one hundred mark. After the second summer the crew and I knew each other so well we could tell when one of us was in a bad mood and solve it with a smile and a glass of champagne. It was a family affair; I became a part of the crew's family.

Our chef was Basilio Lorono, a Basque and one of the personalities of Almadén. He looked natural in either a beret or a chef's tall hat. He could spin tales about learning to tie grape stakes at the age of five in his native Spain or about learning to plant dynamite. He bellowed and he barked — with an accent — he sang and he toasted the ladies while basting chicken with a secret concoction of herbs and seasonings. Sometimes he loaded the steaks with garlic, but no matter. Lorono would recite a Basque proverb something like: "Have another glass of wine and all will be well with the world."

He was past seventy when I met him and had been the vineyard keeper at Novitiate Winery in Los Gatos until they retired him. He picked up his garlic, his secret chicken sauce, and his palate, and moved over to Almadén to the same position. At Los Gatos he tended the few remaining acres of vines and to keep himself active oversaw the gardens, both the flowers and vegetables, and worried about the egg gathering from the partridge, quail and doves. And he became the barbeque chef.

Almadén had done well by Lorono. Until 1959 there were about two hundred acres on the grounds and another thousand nearby and he brought forth the best from them. In fact, it was Lorono who should be given credit for discovering Paicines in the early 1950s. He told Mr. B about the soil there, after he had felt it, smelled it, sniffed it and (probably) tasted it. It was just right for top varietal grapes and later experts from the Viticulture Department at the University of California at Davis confirmed his beliefs.

As time passed and Paicines proved a veritable gold mine as the world's largest single holding of varietals, Basilio was told by Benoist that he would never be forgotten, materially, for his good judgment when he retired; but it never came. Today, Lorono, the old Basque, isn't cynical. He realizes that Benoist was retired before he was and that new companies aren't prone (or expected) to honor the promises made between friends that never found their way onto paper.

Lorono's beautiful golden-haired daughter, Maria, saw to it that I didn't have to worry about the service, the laundry being collected, the glasses kept sparkling, the chipped dishes being used (except in times of crisis), or about finding a place to get away for a few moments to sip champagne in peace (she had a cane chair placed behind the refrigerator!). Al, Mike and Bob Mendizabal, Maria's sons, took care of the guests (and me) and when we needed more help we had only to call on Maria's daughters-in-law, Betty, Maria and Linda.

It was a winning team and our barbeques became the talk of the wine-tasting public in California and the envy of not a few wineries who wished they could furnish such gracious afternoons while garnering the tremendous word of-mouth publicity we received. We sold no wines on the premises, but if we had had retail sales, we would have boomed. We did furnish the names of liquor stores in the vicinity where our wines could be purchased and, as proof of our success, I received many phone calls from liquor store owners and managers requesting a tour because they had heard so much about the winery.

When guests arrived I would give a tour and follow it, depending upon the size of the group, with about forty-five minutes of drinking champagne. Lunch, besides food, allowed four different wines for eight people. After dessert, which was usually fresh fruit and cookies accompanied by newly-ground coffee, we served sherry or port. It was a four- to five-hour afternoon in a relaxing setting for the guests. I usually enjoyed each group, but after five months of continuously greeting people, going through the same routine, and being sociable, I began to look pretty wan and it became a strain to "joyously" entertain the groups booked for the last three months.

My tour was basically the same for all, with added bits of information I had acquired thrown in for the seriously interested. I used elementary psychology and a little acting in order to reach the various types of people I met. I became adept at the job. Within ten minutes I could tell whether corny jokes were the fare, whether I should be serious, or whether to play it somewhat snooty or playful. But most often I found that bubbling enthusiasm for wine was what newcomers wanted most.

Sometimes people out for a drive would see all the cars at the vineyard and stroll in to join the party. Most of the time the boys would report their presence to me because they gave themselves away immediately when they asked what was going on. I would explain that they had joined a private party and invite them for a glass of champagne before leaving. This way they didn't feel insulted and soon left. It was convenient to ask them to walk through the gardens with glass in hand and they felt they were being given preferential treatment at the same time that I had separated them from the private group. Often they could catch sight of Torres in his colorful Mexican attire, with an enormous fiesta sombrero, galloping the horses through the vineyard. This little show gave the uninvited a zestful feeling while it also provided the horses some exercise, which they needed to keep from becoming fat in the lazy, contented atmosphere.

After entertaining a few thousand people of diverse cultural and economic backgrounds, I was prepared for any personality, including the psychiatrist who wanted me to help with his personal problems, the few visitors who became obnoxious from overdrinking or who believed they weren't being given enough wine, or parents who brought their young children to a party designed for adults.

When it was the children who were the problem, I really had more trouble handling Lorono, whose Basque temper rose when he found children picking the wine grapes, playing ball in the vineyards, falling against the tender young vines, or throwing stones at the pheasants. I would give him a straight shot of Scotch, take a glass of champagne myself and wish I could give the kids a big glass so they would go to sleep.

It was a hectic afternoon when the parents of three children, ages six to ten, found their little loved ones missing. I should have known something was amiss because they hadn't been running into the cooking area every five minutes asking for more soft drinks, water, magazines, candy, or bread and their constant questioning had ceased.

The vineyard was searched, the grounds were searched, I even looked inside my house expecting the worst. Then a guest, who had gone to his car for a few moments, saw outside the parking lot by the entrance gates a most unusual sight: several adults milling about children who were selling bunches of Pinot Chardonnay, Pinot Noir, Johannisberg Riesling and Grenache Rosé for five cents a bunch. At the prices those grapes were fetching per ton, they should have been sold for 10 cents per grape and, if Lorono would have had his way, kids, grapes, and parents would be swept out en masse. Instead, he made it a short working day, went home and, I'm sure, partook of something much stronger than wine.

Looking back over the tours I gave I think my biggest headache came when I found out, just three days in advance, that someone's senses had taken a vacation in the San Francisco office and two parties were due at the vineyards simultaneously. Both had arranged for their visit weeks before and a cancellation was out of the question. I had to smooth the egos and juggle the acts.

Having both groups at once was physically possible but not practical. Neither group wanted to join the other, because, after all, they had counted on a private visit for some time and had verified it all by letter. After much cajoling I arranged for one group that was previously to show at noon to come at 10:00 A.M. for the tour, with an 11:00 A.M. champagne hour. The other group, which was originally booked for 1:00 P.M., compromised on a 2:30 P.M. tour and a 3:30 P.M. party.

By 3:00 P.M., most of the first group had gone and my staff changed clothes, reset the tables, cleaned the chairs and benches and uncorked more wine. Meanwhile I was giving the second tour and worrying. When we arrived for the party everything and everyone looked fresh, ready for the guests. The consensus of both groups was a "great" day. But for Al, Mike, Bob, Maria, et al, and myself, it was a twelve-hour day and we had no desire for a return engagement.

There were other days with just as much excitement. It was not unusual for a special group to come for a tour and drinks on the Benoists' terrace while another party was going on at my place. All I had to do was play hostess to both. I did pretty well considering I don't have the gift of bilocation.

The closest we ever came to having a big fight was when a Naval Academy party was being held on one side of the courtyard and an Air Force Academy party was going on on the other. Naturally, it was over football. The two cadets who started it quickly found volunteers for front-line action and we had a melee on the way. But a truce was called over champagne (served by the prettiest faces we could muster) and we didn't have to play the National Anthem.

Because Louie had a naval background, we entertained a great number of Navy men, including some of the highest-ranking officers in the country. In fact, at one party I hosted, the lowest-ranking man present was a full commander. I wanted to ask him how he managed to be included and if he was uncomfortable but thought I had best forego the query. There was so much brass present I had serious concerns for the country's security if a national emergency arose. (Fortunately they didn't have to worry about driving back to headquarters; they all had chauffered cars — complete with rank markings — except the poor commander.)

One of the guests at that party made international headlines not too long ago. Not for his activity at the party, but because he was a part of the news. In this case it was Rear Admiral Chester R. Bender (Commander of the Western Area and the 12th Coast Guard District), now a full admiral and Commandant of the U.S. Coast Guard. In hearing TV and reading newspaper accounts, I sympathized with him and his charming wife at the distress they must have suffered over the sad incident of Simas Kudirka, the Lithuanian who had jumped from a Soviet ship pleading to be kept aboard the Coast Guard vessel *Vigilant*. Through a horrible mix-up in communications he was given back to the Russians, and the pain of a merciless beating and a certain unhappy future.

Over the years there were a number of luncheons given at Almadén for Stanford University bigwigs and their guests. One of them was for Robert Ellsworth Miller, now Director of the USIA's Foreign Press Center, who was then Stanford's assistant University Relations Director and was on his way to becoming Chief of Manpower Development Staff for USIA. Lyle Nelson, his ex-boss, saw to it that guests brought amusing and practical gifts for the Miller's hundred-year-old home in Virginia, such as a keg of nails, a fire extinguisher, rat chasers and a plumber's helper (which I still have pictures of, as Bob held it in one hand with a glass of champagne in the other).

Sometimes those who give, get. Once when we entertained about seventy Republican women, the normal luncheon, tour, and guest speakers were offset by a very dictatorial woman, busty, about sixty-five, who found a never-ending list of things to complain about. She was hoity-toity, ever letting us poor working folk know she was used to much better fare. At her calmest moments she was nothing less than a nuisance. And I didn't even get a chance to bid her a fond farewell.

About 10:00 A.M. the next morning my doorbell rang and

there stood a strange man and the familiar visage of that dame. They wanted to know if we had found any lost "belongings." It wasn't unusual for people to forget gloves, coats, or sunglasses so I asked just what was missing. Her husband replied; she for once was hesitant to speak: "Did you find any dentures? My wife lost a partial."

"No. But I'll look. Where did she lose it?" I asked while giving her a saccharine smile.

No answer from the female half, but her husband said: "Oh, somewhere around the front of your house where she parked the car."

"Really?"

Finally the silent one spoke: "I threw up."

I wanted to laugh, but I expressed sympathy for our formerly superior guest. I looked for the gardener since he might have found the partial while cleaning up. Between my Spanish and José's English, he understood. He had uncovered the partial earlier — considered it cut-rate (no gold) — hosed it off, and placed it where it could easily be found on the hedge. The lady got her denture and summoned up a whispered "thank you." Aside, I suggested that she might give him something so she came across with a dollar and silently left with her husband.

If we can believe television commercials, some people get to sleep counting sheep. I count barbeques . . . The Palo Alto JC's, the San Jose Women's Guild, the Newcomers Club of Sunnyvale, Pan American World Airways' Management Group, Hyatt House employees, the American Association of University Women, the Lockheed Missile Space Company, the University of Denver Club, the Scottish Rite of Santa Cruz, the Junior World Trade Association of San Francisco . . . Zzzzzzzzzzzzzzzzzzz.

CHAPTER VI

MEN I WON'T FORGET

Any feminine female seeking male plaudits should find her ego nurtured, nourished and on cloud nine if she is hostess at a famous winery. I did and I loved almost every moment of it.

I believe it is a man's world and will ever (unless human nature changes and, say, frogs become peacocks) continue to be so.

Being a woman in a man's world can be glamorous, rewarding, frustrating, frightening. Because of my innate carefree nature, I chose it to be glamorous, fun and hopefully (sometimes it was) rewarding. I gave as much effort as any male executive would to a job but I enjoyed it more. I was not consciously seeking a vice-presidency and therefore weighing every word and move and decisively judging whether or not a certain group was worth fifteen more minutes. As long as I had the time, and I saw they were enjoying themselves, they had my time.

I enjoyed making my guests feel at home. I enjoyed being the only female greeter on a vineyard in California and having some men visitors preen and strut and flirt when I gave them special attention. It was a novelty for those who visited many vineyards to find a young woman taking them about and treating them with special consideration.

San Jose State and former Olympic track coach, Bud

Winter, came into my life because of insomnia. A childhood friend told me about a man whom he had heard lecture on the secrets of relaxing. The speaker had taught some fifty thousand Marines how to sleep while guns were firing and planes bombing, so that each hour of rest, before they had to do battle again, would count. The wizard of sleep was called Bud Winter.

Through our mutual friend I talked Bud into coming over to my house. He did — with wife Helen. The actual session lasted about forty-five minutes: half an hour talking to me about various ways to get to sleep and the rest of the time spent while I was prone on a couch (with wife Helen looking on) while Bud verbally hypnotized me into relaxing. "You're lying in a canoe. It's late afternoon, drowsily warm but not hot. You're stretching, you're so contented, you're hearing the languid lap of the water against the sides of the boat, your eyes are getting heavy-lidded, you don't care what happens to the world right at that moment, if only you can just rest, relax, sleep, sleep, sleep. . . ."

We went through several idyllic scenes and finally I was so sleepy, all I wanted to do was get them both out of my living room so I could go to bed. They left, I slept. And it was the last time the lessons worked. Helen explained that it was great if someone talked to you, but if you tried to talk yourself into sleep, well . . . .

But my friendship with Bud and Helen goes on.

From the 1968 Olympics in Mexico City, where Bud was to see his athletes in glory (and some think infamy for the U.S. because of Tommie Smith and John Carlos and their black power salute while receiving their medals), I got this card:

Dear Mary,

Once again it is the human interest, the color stories, and the story behind the story that makes the Olympics. San Jose State won four gold and one bronze medal and Chris [Papanicolaou, who in 1970 pole vaulted 18′ ¼″ for a world record] vaulted 17′ 6½″ for a 4th [place] and only three countries in the world beat that. Will tell all when I see you.

Bud

Certainly one of the greatest track coaches in the U.S. as well as having trained as many, if not more champions, than any living track mentor, Bud found the 1968 Olympics behind-the-scenes acts quite tiring even for his relaxed temperament. Some of his athletes were harrassed politically by their own team-mates to such an extent that only hours before a race in which one of Bud's men was expected to cop the gold, the young man had disappeared. Newsmen, who had been relentlessly questioning him as to whether or not he would make the black power salute if he won, or would he wear colors or insignia showing his allegiance, forced him to flee. He showed up in Bud's room to that man's surprise. But relief wasn't to be found just then as the sorrowful and perplexed runner literally sobbed out his problems in Bud's arms. He didn't want to get involved in politics. He wanted only to run but he had been told that running was not enough: he had to show political colors, otherwise he was betraying his fellow black men.

He wanted to run for himself, for his country, for his school, for his coach, for his family. He didn't want to get involved.

A peak of Bud's counseling career was at hand. He soothed, consoled, the young man but explained that only he could decide what he should do.

Until the actual event four hours later, Bud did not know if the track star would show up. Appear he did and won another gold medal for the U.S. As for Bud, several grey hairs came in double strength.

I'd been around enough Europeans and Englishmen so as not to be immediately bowled over by their ingrained-through-the-centuries charm. Nonetheless, several I met at the vineyard were extraordinarily debonair and I had to force myself to play it cool since, after all, I was selling wine.

Two Englishmen, Peter Noble and Terry Tofield, arrived one Sunday afternoon after a drive from San Francisco. They had planned on staying and chatting with me for about an hour, but ended up leaving some six or more hours later, after joining the barbeque held that afternoon.

The day turned out as Peter said, "a smashing success."

Peter, head of the four-hundred-year-old firm Christopher & Co., Ltd., Wine Merchants, wanted to see if Almadén's Blanc de Blancs could be handled by his firm in England and if we might be able to import his company's Scotch.

If I had had the say-so, I would have let Peter's firm handle every product, especially after a few hours of Peter's and Terry's company. These two men are tops in their salesmanship.

Terry is export manager for the firm and I found myself going through a bit of history reading the brochures they left. Christopher & Co. started during the reign of Elizabeth I and since then they have been entitled to say: "By Appointment to H.M. Queen Elizabeth" or "H.M. King etc." They are one of only two or three spirits firms who can still claim that privilege.

I sent both of these gallants pictures I took of them, glass of champagne in hand, lounging against the hood of their rented car. And, I was assured, that is not the reason they are now doing business with Christian Brothers.

Any girl looking for the physical personification of what the Prince in *Cinderella* or *Snow White* should resemble, would find her dream fulfilled upon meeting Christian Pol-Roger, scion of the champagne house of Pol-Roger, Epernay, France.

Blond, aristocratic, so handsome I immediately regretted the fact he was younger than I. It took only a few minutes around Christian and I began visualizing him as a young officer in the Confederate Army (I figured if Lafayette could help Washington do battle, surely there were Frenchmen in the War Between the States) riding up to my plantation door. I had actually thought of making the horse a palomino but realized that I was not playing the role of "Ramona" but a Southern belle.

Although Christian spoke good English, I was certain he thought in French and, thankfully, therefore, couldn't read my thoughts. After he left, with the president and division manager of W.A. Taylor & Co., his distributors, I made the effort to purchase a case of Pol-Roger. And found the color of the wine almost the color of his hair.

There was one Frenchman I could have done without. Young, a Count and part of a family who'd been in the wine business for centuries, he was a guest of the Benoists. Two hours of conversation after dinner and the Benoists decided to call it a night. Rather than suggest the young man likewise get some sleep, Mr. B said, "Mary, here, will take you to her place and entertain you."

Such statements always jolted me. They were innocent enough but had connotations, especially to foreigners. I suspect Louie Benoist delighted in seeing my reaction as well as that of the men present.

Taking the Count by the hand, we went into the special tasting room quarters I had, rooms that were at one end of the house. Over a glass of Blanc de Blancs we chatted as well as possible with his limited English and my French. Within minutes, I found we were holding hands, five minutes and one glass later he was stroking my left arm, seconds more and the strokes were ricocheting in all directions. "No, no. *Non, non! Cherie!*" My exclamations only stirred the Romeo onward. Due partly to the precarious slant of the table and wobbly three-legged chairs, I found myself dumped onto the sisal flooring with would-be conqueror half on top of me.

My "please let me up" pleadings were to no avail and the overly stimulated young man was now obviously determined. So was I. Falling on the floor, he had hit a small stand causing a candlestick holder in the form, naturally, of grape clusters, to drop and lose its candle.

Frantically I grabbed the holder, blindly swung and then surveyed the scene. No doubt but the Count was down for the count. I dared to kneel beside him. He was breathing. "Thank God I haven't killed him. But what to do? I can't call my mother as she will surely have a heart attack. The Benoists? Tell them about their guest? What an embarrassing situation!"

Feeling Florence Nightingalish, I mistakenly began patting his face and whispering, "Poor darling, I really didn't mean to hurt you."

Then, this time I found myself in a stranglehold with the sly pretender. There was again no kidding about his intentions and moments counted. Suddenly, remembering everything the nuns hadn't taught me, I jammed a strong knee into him and let lengthy fingernails rip. Instinctively I found myself on my feet, forgetting about torn nylons.

A minute later, the Count was operative but his directional signals were not geared for my direction. As he left, he did have the last word, "You're not a woman; a true woman would not have struggled. She would have known love."

I smiled, I said, "Good night." I realized then how young he really was and I wondered how suddenly his English was quite understandable.

The next afternoon we met in the courtyard. He was leaving that day. As a memento, I gave him a first edition of a book he had admired. He said, simply, "*Merci.*"

After this episode I was wary about being alone, secluded, with a male guest. Then again, after some months and meeting many more wonderful men, I relaxed my guard and, luckily, found no more upsetting scenes.

A foreign visitor who had felt graciously entertained at Almadén would tell his fellow friends and countrymen and often I would be hostessing groups of three to forty men representing news media, farming, industry, politics, from Europe, South America, England. I particularly enjoyed getting in political discussions with these men. And, as a private citizen, even the U.S. State Department did not mind my questioning the visitors and they, likewise, getting my viewpoints on various matters.

It was love at first sight upon meeting Dr. Raul Fernandez of the Chamber of Deputies of Argentina. In his 60s, a gentleman, cultured, learned, filled with so much wisdom that he understood all the foibles of human nature; I had the compulsion to rub my fingers across his strong-featured, pock-marked face. He and five other deputies (comparable to our Senators) stayed in my living room delving as deeply into every aspect of today's living as two hours after lunch would afford us until the limousines came to take them back to San Francisco.

Just before departing, Señor Fernandez kissed me on the cheek and a photographer caught the scene. I have the newspaper photo, and the few mailings from him I cherish.

Another caballero near the equatorial line was Renato Almeida, seventy-two-year old head of Brazil's cultural affairs and his country's top advisor to UNESCO. It was on, supposedly, a day off when Dr. Almeida came for about two hours and stayed about six. We danced the tango, sang, talked, ate, sipped champagne. I presented him with one of Frank Schoonmaker's books and he gave me a typical Carrioca rag doll of Brazil's *favelas*.

There were quite a number of freeloaders. You could seldom tell for sure until approximately an hour had passed. Then, it was hard to suddenly bid them goodby without being very undiplomatic. One Chilean Congressman from a wine growing area insisted on seeing Almadén. Seven hours later I thought I might well have a perennial guest on my hands. At my own expense I gave him brunch, lunch, wine, cognac, but told the State Department interpreter I was not going to host a dinner for him. The poor escort had a touchy matter; he couldn't be heavy-handed with the visitor as there were country-to-country relations involved as well as his standing a chance of losing his job.

Since it was a question of my day off which I had given up again as well as my food and hospitality, I made the move and said to the Congressman, "Before you leave in the next few minutes, would you care to take as a gift a bottle of champagne and a red or white wine?" Then, after he made his choice, I ushered him and the escort (who was, he said, eternally grateful to me) out to the car.

Exactly four months later I received, in the line of thanks, a mimeographed form letter from the Chilean. Next time I heard from the escort-interpreter, he said that, after taking the Congressman all over the U.S. for three weeks, he had never again heard from him.

But, most of the men VIPs were joys for me to show around. When introduced to Dr. Paul Buck, head of the feeding program for the astronauts, I said, "Any relation to Frank?" He'd evidently heard that many times and came right back with a quotable quip. "I don't just aim for bringing 'em back alive. I make sure, with a good diet, they're happy about it." Paul explained to me in language I could understand, the diet of the astronauts, and gave me cubes of the various foods. He believes in wine as a food and it was recently announced that the astronauts will now be able to sip a bit of medium dry sherry when in space.

After a time, the snobbism in me begged that I meet some Italians, members of the aristocracy, dating back further than Garabaldi. But socializing with such people during their stay in the U.S. meant they had to come to me. And so one did. By name of the Marchesi Lodovico Antinori, member of the famous Chianti family which started producing wine in Florence in the fourteenth century.

Lodovico was brought to the vineyard by a representative for Julius Wile Sons & Co., as far as I'm concerned, one of the three or four great import firms in the U.S. Lodovico was a combination of the best of any Italian film star. Although in his mid-twenties, he had the innate experience of centuries of pleasing women and his fellow man. Watching him talking, flirting, it was suddenly easy to understand why sometimes a man years younger than a woman really isn't younger.

I think Florentine Italians are elegant, virile, forceful. Lodovico gave me pictures of his family home, drew an arrow to the room where he was born, explained Chianti wines to me, conversed and looked at me as if I were the only woman in the world. I loved every minute of it and only wished I could witness a day in his life when back in Florence.

Besides my finding him *fantastico*, I found his wines to be excellent. And, since my mother discovered they are some of the Pope's favorites, I've had to buy cases with my own lira. Now, whenever I see an Antinori on a wine menu, I'll order it. Such was the charm — and the wines — of Lodovico.

Some of the men I shall never forget were winemakers and the best — Mike Bo, who used to work for Almadén and was the guiding light at San Martin Winery; George Thoukis, a top winemaker at Gallo; Al Huntsinger, the fine winemaster of Almadén; Norbert Mirassou of the Mirassous; and Dick Vine, who has his own Niagara Falls Winery — these were some whose company I relished.

Sitting by my fireplace, after hours, and talking shop while trying out a new blend, was the epitome of happiness. Instead of having to read scholarly articles by these masters of their profession, I had the distinction of being in their presence, in a friendly socializing where, in our own respective fields, we felt equal and yet were eager to learn from each other and to impart any bit of knowledge anyone else present requested.

An hour of question and answer session with Al or Mike or George provided me with more information on wines than fifteen hours of study. Even with the familiarity of seeing some of the greats of the wine world congregating in my house, I still was very much aware that it was a unique relationship, and one to be treasured.

Walter Taylor, of the Taylor wine company family (and now the owner of Bully Hill Vineyards in Hammondsport, N.Y.), snuck into my circle of wine making friends when he and his then wife, Ellen, came as ordinary walk-in visitors to the winery late one winter afternoon. They didn't introduce themselves but asked so many technical and pertinent questions, that I finally asked if they were in the wine industry.

Once identified, we really began to establish a rapport and Walter and Ellen and I spent several hours together chatting about mutual acquaintances and, naturally, wines. Karl Wente had to be phoned and notified that the Taylors would be very late arriving at his winery.

But, it wasn't until a wine convention that I found out from

Dick Vine (how could any winemaker have a better name?) that Walter's nickname is "Falcon." I even made out a check to "Falcon" when I ordered a copy of his and Dick's *Home Winemaker's Handbook*, a book so simply stated and easily understood that many winemakers wish they had beat these men in publishing. My check came back but not because it had bounced. It was their gift to me. Walter didn't know that Dick told me the name had been given him when, as a young, flamboyant ideaman, he would often show up at office meetings with a gloved hand and arm and a hooded falcon perched thereon.

Unforgettable are the men of the Raventós family in Barcelona, Spain, makers of an outstanding champagne called Codorniu. The family has to be memorable — there are so many of them it is impossible to say, "I can't recall that name." All are endowed with charisma seldom found in such abundance that when a cablegram was read to me in Spanish over the phone at 6:00 A.M. (the middle of my night) asking when the white grapes would be picked, I beat back any sarcasm and answered cheerfully.

It was 1964 when Jesús Raventós and a nephew, Manuel Pagés Raventós, arrived on the scene at Almadén. Jesús, about 60, and Manuel came as walk-ins. They knew they wanted to visit Almadén (after all it was named after a quicksilver mine in Spain), but had neglected to make their intentions known to our head office.

From my initial meeting with these advance charmers of the House of Codorniu, a friendship developed that still endures. I have since entertained and enjoyed the company of so many Raventós that, even with the booklet given me containing a diagram of the family tree, I'm not sure who is who. All I know is that Jesús Raventós, if he were not already married, is the man I would most want as a suitor. Pau Raventós Artés has a great personality and speaks the best English. Daniel Pagés Raventós is single and, therefore, after some members of his family looked my way, poor Daniel became a bit edgy. But I was fortunate to be able to give Daniel a birthday party on one of his visits with Pau and Manuel. Daniel is shy — around single women. His relatives think this is a Spanish trait; it is not.

There have been other Raventós and wives. And, someday, if I ever get to use my renewed passport, I should love to visit Barcelona as surely there will be ten or fifteen Raventós waiting to entertain me as well as a great champagne which they have been making for over one hundred years.

Taking around television teams working on documentaries can be a bore. Showing Ed Newman the works was a fun thing. He was producing and narrating a film on wineries in California because at that time the Bear State was making waves by taking away sales from New York and Europe.

It was so easy to work with Ed. He is a pro, period.

After his day's work was completed, we went to San Francisco for dinner. In the rental car, heading back to the vineyard, I tried giving directions. Consequently I got him lost. I guess, to calm his nerves, as well as get correct directions, we stopped for a drink at the nearest place off the freeway, the unbelievable "Last Chance Bar."

Ed is a true, without show-offishness, gourmet. His mother taught him how valuable good food is to the body as well as how delightful it can be to the palate. After listening to his sincere yak, I can say that he has become one of my favorite wine connossieurs in the communications media. He is a gentleman of any cultured school of thought and a wit to boot. I caught him in a recent picture in *House Beautiful* (giving his favorite recipes) wearing a black-with-white-stripes apron of the old-fashioned French butcher. But Ed can cope with the apron as well as many more affairs of world importance. He is a perfectionist.

An oddity in anybody's world was the man who sent me a threatening note and an obscene color snapshot with the warning that I'd best meet with him or —

That piece of mail sent me into temporary shock, but I quickly remembered advice on what to do in just such a case, and phoned the Sheriff's department. Within minutes a deputy was questioning me and looking at the evidence.

We set a trap. My phone lines were tapped to get any incoming calls in answer to my come-hither "personal" ad in both local papers. Within two days of my placing the ad I received over forty-five calls ranging from men who thought they were rediscovering an old flame or an ex-wife, to a kook who was looking for an extra thrill. But, not the recognizable voice of the man who had phoned the same day I received the letter.

On the fourth day of suspense, he called. Attempting to put

on an Oscar-winning performance, I promised to meet him at the spot he suggested.

He was a no-show.

Another two weeks and the tap went off as well as most of the nervousness. But it took almost three months before the case was solved. Picked up on a Peeping Tom charge was a twenty-eight-year-old grocery clerk. He had, in his car, a paper box file of newspaper pictures and clips of women throughout the area. I was one of them. The same man had been writing obscene letters and making threatening calls to the wife of a vice president of the grocery chain for which he worked. There were four other women, whom he had also intimidated, listed in the copies of his letters and photo album.

It was a sickening experience for me.

But, being young, naive and trusting, I soon forgot my ordeal and eagerly looked forward to the next group of fascinating men to visit the vineyard.

CHAPTER VII

NOTORIETY

I have always been used to being around the acclaimed. But I did not expect to be thrust into fame as a woman in the wine world.

However, finding myself somewhat of a known personality was exciting and at times gave me a heady feeling.

Because of my unusual job, I was asked to be the "real" Mary Lester on the national TV show *To Tell the Truth*. Mort Greene, prize-winning songwriter, intellectual wit, writer of the difficult pantomime segment of Red Skelton's long-running TV show, thought I'd make a good subject for his network's celebrity guessing program. The producer agreed and I was flown to New York to try to outwit Kitty Carlisle, Peggy Cass, and Orson Bean as the panelists, while Bud Collyer was the host.

So many people asked me whether the show was rigged. Emphatically no. The permanent panelists absolutely do not know who the real authority is. The producer and assistant producer do know. And I believe Bud Collyer did. At least I had that impression. But certainly not the star-studded questioners.

The "celebrity guests" surely earn any penny they might make by winning. We three girls put in almost two full eight-hour days practicing the acting routine and getting briefed on the particular subject for that show.

I went over and over and over with the two false Mary
Lesters the basic information they should know about California wines. (On the show they could lie but I had to tell the
truth.) Both of the girls knew something about wine but one
was familiar only with European varieties.

The outcome of our talk sessions was that we stumped the
panel and won the $1000, thereby entitling each of us to
$333.33. I got a thank-you letter from the producer and
$333.34. The note and extra penny are in a frame hanging
alongside other mementoes, on a hallway wall.

I had been somewhat turned off by show biz personalities
since my early teens when I had sent away for a picture of Gary
Cooper and received a form letter from the studio requesting a
quarter.

Bud Collyer turned me on. He was so sincere and had such
warmth that even the most nontrusting would recognize him as
a nonphoney. At the end of the show, Bud kissed me and I
didn't want to wash my face that night. I later did some
inquiring and found that he was a loved show business figure
and I wasn't the only stranger to him who, within minutes, felt
like a friend.

That TV program brought me mail from people I hadn't
heard from in years. Wine dealers and restaurant owners wanted
to have me do guest appearances for them and I was asked to
lecture and appear on other radio and TV shows. Most all had
to be turned down.

While in New York City for *To Tell the Truth*, there was
a champagne reception given for me which retailers and
restaurateurs citywide attended. I especially remember it as it
was held in the beautiful showrooms of Frederick Wildman
Import Firm and it rained that afternoon as heavily as it does in
the Canal Zone. I remember it also because I had hoped to
deliver in person two bottles of champagne to William Buckley
who was then campaigning for mayor of New York. Bill wasn't
in his offices but his sister, Priscilla, promised she would get the
bubbly to him if I could get it to her. I could barely make out
the figure of the doorman at the South Sutton Place apartment
address, the rain was so thick. My hero, Bill, did get the wine,
though, as he sent me a note in appreciation adding that he and
his wife, Pat, particularly enjoyed drinking it while watching the
election results — it helped diminish the sting of the outcome.

And, a couple of years later, while in the beauty salon at the Beverly Wilshire Hotel in Beverly Hills, a voice emanating from the next booth asked, "Will the real Mary Lester please stand up?"

It was one of the girls who'd been on the show with me and she had recognized my voice as well as catching a glimpse of me in a mirror. Anyway, the hairdresser was impressed.

I looked forward to being on the *Gypsy Rose Lee TV Show* and found it disappointing. If I had known that at that time Gypsy was quite ill, I would have been more understanding of her brusque ways. As it was, I thought her quite rude and very "on" throughout the taping. Charles Beard, the cooking expert, was also to be on the show. I got as much biography on Beard as possible, and read up on specific wine matters the producer said I'd probably be asked.

It was while the makeup man was pancaking me that I discovered the entire show format and guests had been switched. I introduced myself to the man standing behind me waiting his turn to be powdered, and then asked his name. This, I instinctively sensed, was not the right opening gambit. His short, terse reply: "Paul Lynde." I had never heard of him but gathered I should have. The other guest was, as far as I'm concerned, the female counterpart in graciousness to Bud Collyer, none other than Betty White. I wondered how she felt without Macy's or Tournament of Roses Parade background scenery.

Before the program, I spent a few minutes with Gypsy, chatting and asking where I could have a case of champagne sent to her. I also wondered aloud if she remembered some twenty years back when playing the St. Charles Theater (then also Minsky's) in New Orleans and a young newspaper reporter came to her dressing room for an interview, sat down on a sofa laden with pillows and immediately leaped across the room at the sound of a banshee "yip! yip!" and her screams. He had sat on her Mexican hairless.

Gypsy remembered, and I explained that I knew about the scene as the reporter was my eldest brother. She smiled, and I figured the show would be fun.

It wasn't for me. It became a game of ad-libbing and quick sharp repartee between Lynde and Gypsy. Since I wasn't getting paid, and my company would have been flabbergasted if for once in my life I'd kept my mouth shut, I felt I had to talk as rapidly as possible whenever possible. It wasn't too often, but I managed.

As a souvenir of my appearance I was given a small butane cigarette lighter etched with the name Gypsy Rose Lee. I gave it to my mother. The following day it broke and was tossed out. I do have a tape of the show, though, to remind me never to take on a pro unless I am likewise a pro in that field.

One speaking engagement I regret not being able to honor. It was an invitation to be the dinner speaker at the annual convention in Monterey of Hospital Directors of the Western States. The previous year they had had Abigail Van Buren and the year before Ivy Baker Priest. I was told each year they tried to get not just a woman with an unusual occupation, but a speaker who was witty. To have been placed in such elite company with the previous speakers was almost as flattering to me as a proposal from the right man.

And, at that particular time, the idea of following Abby ran a little deeper in my thoughts than merely an after-dinner talk.

Abby's column was then being syndicated by McNaught Syndicate. Her contract was soon to expire and both she and the powers at McNaught were at odds on the terms for a new contract. Charlie McAdam, Sr., then president of the syndicate, asked me to write some sample columns. Just in case Abby split with them, they wanted to have an advice columnist on hand. So, between general tours, special tours, barbeques, VIP visitors and trying to remember what day it was, for a month I read and reread reams of Dear Abby copy, fabricated about one hundred questions and then answered them.

My sample columns were handed around to various members of the McNaught staff, only one of whom knew me personally, and then I was sent the remarks of the individuals.

Pretty good. Well written. Much livelier than the average advice column. Falls short of the cynical, flippant, occasionally humorous and off-color quips of Abby. But some papers that don't like Abby's fresh style might prefer this one. Has this writer been using Abby's questions?

Sounds like Abby. I think well-done especially if the writer also wrote the questions.

Generally good imitation of Abby's style. Some of

answers could be sharper, shorter — others as good as Abby's answers.

My reward was getting that off-the-cuff criticism and knowing that at least I had been asked to try to follow such an act. Abby did switch syndicates, McNaught decided not to have a replacement for her, and I'm still wondering how to utilize all those original questions and answers reposing in a manila envelope.

Being recognized can have its drawbacks. After two or three years of entertaining and touring visiting restaurant owners, bar managers, liquor store buyers, and maître d's, there were few popular restaurants or bars where I could go without having one of the staff members greet me. I enjoyed the hospitality, but sometimes it was distressing. Particularly when with a date I'd been turning down for weeks with the excuse of being too busy to go out, and then have the maître d' greet me as if I'd been dining there three times weekly for the past month. And, alas, my mother never could understand why I seemed to know, by first name yet, so many bartenders.

Once, to get a respite from vineyard life, I took my mother for a few days to the Pine Inn in Carmel. We made the dining room just before closing time. Jockeying to serve us was a young man who didn't look familiar, but who addressed me by name. He explained that he had gone to the Monterey Peninsula College training facility for restaurant personnel and had come with a group of trainees to Almadén where I had given them a special tasting and tour. He also stated that since then he had never had a drop of wine. Not knowing how I was supposed to react, I smiled and toyed with the silver, while he continued with the story.

He confessed he had never before had any wine and the idea of freeloading was too good to resist, especially since he could barely afford to buy one beer each week. So he tried to drink as much as he could during the visit and finished off part of a bottle on the bus ride back. This darn near finished him as well. He was so sick that, until days later, he couldn't even bring himself to read the notes he'd taken. "But," he assured me, smiling, "I'm convinced all the good things you said about wine are true and I sell lots of it. But none for me."

The U.S. Navy, via Moffett Field, bestowed on me the title of Honorary Commander of a Lockheed P3A Orion, a submarine chaser. On the appointed day, I was hosted by Commander Joe Lapham, acting on behalf of his boss, the Admiral, and given a welcoming speech. Then, escorted by Commander Lapham and several of his officers to one of the actual P3As, I was blindfolded before entering the cabin. The men simply would not understand that I couldn't tell one piece of radar from another and they were taking no chances of my reporting what I'd seen.

After a tour of the gigantic hangar where the blimps used to be berthed, a brief ceremony ensued and I was presented a hand-carved wooden replica of the plane. I was also instructed to guard it carefully. Only the squadron commander and the C.O. of the base had these replicas and, consequently, a lot of pilots were itching to own one, even if someone else's. True advice, for before we'd even finished lunch, at the Admiral's table, naturally, I'd had two offers to sell the plane and one not-so-shy man trying to walk off with it.

Being invited for a private tour on board any ship is fun, but being a special guest on board an aircraft carrier and dining in the Captain's cabin is even more fun.

Captain Jack Kenyon, skipper of the U.S.S. *Oriskany*, had me and my escort brother piped aboard. After that splendid afternoon with Captain Kenyon and his crew, I changed allegiance from submarines to aircraft carriers. Sorry, *Nautilus*, you're too confining.

Happiness at becoming a "somebody" meant being elected an Associate Member of the American Society of Enologists. To quote the ASE definition: "A professional society of enologists, viticulturists, and others in the fields of wine and grape production, promoting technical advancement and integrated research in science and industry."

When I received my membership notice from then President Elie Skofis, I felt I really belonged in the "in" group. At that time there were about ten women who had been admitted to this exclusive company, most of them chemists. Today the total membership is about seven hundred with about twenty-five women. A decision between carrying a Blue Cross card or my ASE card would tax me, for sure. I'm so proud of it.

Once a year there is an ASE three-day convention some-place in California, and members come from all over the world to hear talks on the technical aspects of wine and wine making, thoughtfully limited to fifteen minute maximums. And then to enjoy more talk on the not-so-technical aspects of wines, wine making and wine personnel during the after-hours partying. Also, the ASE puts out a very, very intellectual and technical quarterly journal. Once in awhile, though, it will innocently print a scholarly article that proves interesting to the "thumbing through" reader who sees several pages, including graphs, of a treatise such as "Reproductive Response of Japanese Quail Fed Varietal Grapes."

Certainly a reader used to *Playboy* would find most of the articles extremely technical and bland. But sometimes they, inadvertently, are not sterile.

A few years ago the *Holiday* Magazine "Best Restaurants in the U.S. Award" was held in San Francisco. Marlo Mondine, co-owner of the Blue Fox, held a special party in his wine cellar for about two dozen of the award recipients. Most of the guests were from New Orleans where the previous year the awards were given and a private party had been hosted at Brennan's by the Brennans.

For the Blue Fox fete, I was chosen the mystery guest.

I could hardly wait to see John Brennan again and get a look at the girl he'd married. It was to be a dramatic moment for me because as a schoolgirl in New Orleans I had developed a crush on John, then a handsome young Navy aviator whose elder brother, Owen, owned the famous Absinthe House besides the century-old Vieux Carre restaurant, whose name was later changed to Brennan's.

I thought of every excuse possible to visit the Absinthe House when John might be there. I'd carry my schoolbooks into the cubbyhole of an office behind the bar where John's sisters, Ella and Adelaide, did the paperwork and bookkeeping, and ordered supplies from liquor and wine salesmen.

Pretending I was just there to say hello to the girls, I looked for John and took in the sales pitch of the men about their products. My wine knowledge began in New Orleans.

At the Blue Fox party I was quickly recognized by most of the guests. Surprisingly, my heart did not do extraordinary leaps upon seeing John. He was still handsome and gentlemanly, but in the intervening years I had observed other handsome men. So, not courageously but wisely, I concluded that his lovely wife was best for him and I would keep my schoolgirl memories.

Many of the privileges accorded me were rewards for my

working for a special company which had given money to certain private and public events. I was often offered choice tickets to operas and symphonies in San Francisco. And, because Almadén was a sponsor of the San Jose Light Opera Association, I got to watch closely the presentation of *Kismet* which in itself meant little to me, but it featured in a minor part a young girl by the name of Nancy Bonetti. My brother knew her parents, and the senior Bonettis insisted he see Nancy. Luckily I had excellent seats and we observed Nancy at age thirteen or so, exuberantly leaping about. Four or five years later she went on to become one of the original Gold Diggers and was chosen twice to travel with Bob Hope on his Christmas overseas junkets. Nancy is now very much Miss Show Business and a ripe, beautiful twenty-one.

Being acclaimed meant having an *entrée* to the President's box at the Stanford football games where wonderful Lyle Nelson, head of University Relations, handled every ruffle with dignity and, if possible, a laugh. It meant having Dan McGuire, the former PR man for St. Mary's College, Moraga, and the San Francisco 49ers (and whom I hadn't seen since long ago New Orleans days when he was covering the Sugar Bowl festivities), visit me bringing two dozen red roses. I found him just as handsome and personable. It was interesting to learn about his later marriage to Margaret Keene, who with her former husband, Walter, was noted for painting the enormous-eyed waifs of World War II days.

Being "known" meant receiving an I LOVE YOU card spelled out by IBM computer and hundreds of phone calls and letters with very little identification. The letters, especially, were exasperating when signed simply "Bob" or "Tom" or "Jane."

It meant getting mail addressed only: "Mary Lester, Los Gatos, Calif." (I remembered Robert Ruark telling me a proof that he'd become famous was receiving letters: "Robert Ruark, New York City." I reminded myself that Los Gatos had only about ten thousand people and I had likewise endeared myself to the half-dozen postal clerks by gifting them occasionally with bottles of wine.)

One of those epistles I received with only my name and the city was from a gentleman I'd been corresponding with for some fifteen years: Tom Mboya, then Kenya's Minister of Economic Planning and Development, as well as U.N. delegate.

In this letter, written shortly before he was assassinated, Tom said he hoped to be in California in the very near future and was looking forward to visiting me at Almadén. Even before his meteoric rise, I'd been writing him in Kenya and sending cash for his various charitable works in Africa. I had pleaded with him not to follow in Julius Nyerre's radical socialistic footsteps. So, I had watched Tom's career quite closely. While at the Miami *Herald*, the fellows on the copy desk knew of my interest in Dr. Mboya and when he married a lovely African girl who had gone to college in the U.S., there was posted, quite prominently, a UPI photo showing the married couple and printed across it the words: "Lester Jilted."

Tom's murder particularly saddened me. His death meant the loss of a great leader for his country as well as a prophet-politician for all of Africa.

Time Magazine Senior Editor John Scott gave me this problem to solve: he had purchased an entire wine cellar at what he thought a bargain price. But, hopefully, had he bought a prize?

Wanting to stay in John's favor, I quickly contacted Frank Schoonmaker and two other connoisseurs and read off parts of the wine list. The consensus: John had bought himself a fine cellar, nothing fantastic, but certainly worth more than what he'd paid.

I'd been told getting in Herb Caen's column in the San Francisco *Chronicle* was the "most." I made it. Likewise, to my amazement I was featured in a nationally syndicated cartoon "Opinionwise," and that brought letters from newly made fans and friends of long standing.

Other pleasant events: Mario and Tina Mondine of the Blue Fox in San Francisco sent me Blue Fox playing cards and bath powder; I had recipes of mine, my mother's and family cooks (under my name) printed in *Recipes of California Winemakers*; and Louie B. Nunn, then Governor of Kentucky, commissioned me a Kentucky Colonel.

Getting picked to be on the *Sunset* Magazine Taste Panel was a treat. As at all their tastings, the panel of judges for that particular luncheon were considered experienced in food and drink and the ballots given us left little room for quibbling. The ratings were to be: superb, yummy, good, so-so and yuk. Outside of the main rating, there were statements to be made: "I'm a poor judge because I just don't like ____ " and

"Comments? (Is it too sweet, sour, salty, hot, bland, sharp, bitter, soupy, firm?)"

Nothing, absolutely nothing is printed in *Sunset's* recipe section unless one hundred percent of the taste panel agree. In my case, I was the only one who enjoyed the collard greens. I thought they were marvelous because whenever I had had them before they had had the taste of iron licked right off the bar. Collard greens didn't make the magazine recipe list but Shrimp Creole did. It was voted yummy for the tummy.

Notoriety meant having Louise Davies, whose husband, Ralph, was the Chairman of the Board of American President Line, asking if you could attend a party (and maybe say a few words to her guests about wine) at her estate in Woodside or at her Firehouse (an authentic one) in San Francisco. Louise wanted so badly to buy the hundred-and-so-year-old fire engine on the grounds of Almadén. It was a pity to see it just standing there, hoses holey and brass getting brown-green. She believed her Firehouse, the scene of many of San Francisco's most written-about parties, would be a perfect setting for the engine. I ditto that.

What a wonderful feeling to be greeted by name at the reception desk of the Beverly Wilshire and to find that the courtly Don — Hernando Courtright — has seen to it that flowers or fresh fruit or even a bottle of champagne is in your room as a special welcoming greeting.

And I began to believe that I'd really made it when a neighbor's ten-year-old daughter brought me a paper she wrote for classroom homework. It had a big red *A* inked on top. Her subject: "Ten Most Famous Women in the World." Berit Gundersen listed me as the foremost woman authority on wine in the U.S.A.

I immediately decided to sign Berit up as my press agent — she'll be out of school in ten more years.

CHAPTER VIII

HOW IT'S ALL DONE

If it hadn't been for my having the good fortune to have lived on a producing vineyard with a winery a few feet from my back door, I still would be rummaging through countless wine books picking up bits of information here and a few more driblets there. One could read a dozen books without really knowing how the grapes become wine, how the wine gets into the bottle and how wine should be used. Most books on wine are either quite technical or travel-semibiographical articles on various wineries. For conciseness and clarity, some of the booklets put out by the Wine Advisory Board and various individual wineries in the East and West are best bets for learning lots without putting in hours of tedious study.

One of the basic questions asked me by thousands of inquisitive visitors to the winery was: what is wine made from? Everyone seemed to know it was an alcoholic beverage. But what was the base? Dandelions? Cherries? Prunes?

They weren't trying to play guessing games. They were serious in admitting not knowing that wines to be drunk with the meal, commonly known as table wines, come from grapes.

Wines made from grapes go way back to the Greeks and Romans.

To top everything, one of the strangest uses of wine is recounted by the Greek historian Herodotus in his account of a

Persian use of wine:

They drink wine freely, and it is their custom to take counsel on the most serious matters while they are drunk. On the following day the master of the house in which the deliberations took place proposes to them again, while sober, the decision that they reached the night before, and if it is also agreeable to them when sober, they adopt it; if not, they reject it. Furthermore, the conclusions that they first reach when sober, they consider again while drunk.

Sound like a cop out?

The Latins had wine festivals in honor of their own wine god. The Roman priests kept a close surveillance of vineyards and the making of wine. It was they who ruled that only ripe grapes should be pressed and they kept a cautious watch over fermentation. These religious men could very well have been responsible for the discovery that a properly pruned vine makes a much better wine.

To make good wine there must be a good winemaker as well as good grapes. There must also be a good viticulturist. If it's a small winery and vineyard, the winemaker usually decides what grapes to plant, and when he thinks the grapes are ripe he takes samples and has the juice analyzed to see whether there is enough sugar content to bring the alcohol count to the amount needed for a good dry table wine.

In larger wineries such as Christian Brothers, Paul Masson, Beringer, and Almadén, top management decides what kind of grapes they would like to plant. This depends greatly on what kind of wine is selling and whether the vineyards already produce enough or need much more.

The viticulturist has to know if the soil can produce good vines of the particular type needed. He's the man who has to watch the vine from the time it is grafted to the very end when the grapes are picked. In the meantime he is constantly alerting the winemaker as to soil conditions, growth of the vine, maturing of the grapes. But it is the winemaker who makes the final decision when to pick and start transforming the fruit into liquid hospitality.

Long ago, men who owned their own vineyards and made their own wine either for strictly home use or for the marketplace, learned through years of experience and trial and error how to blend wines, age, filter in the best methods, store, etc. Some of them even had chemistry experience and found that test tubes and scientific analysis were a great help along with their natural taste buds and workaday experience. Their knowledge and expertise they passed along to their sons and their sons' sons, and so the reputations of wineries were built.

But for the past thirty or thirty-five years to be a fine "old-fashioned" winemaker is not enough; the winemaker must also be an enologist. This means he must have scientific training, schooling in all phases of wine making as well as actual on-the-job training. He must be a professional.

There are few enology schools in the world. The one that would accumulate the most votes of greatness from winemasters worldwide would be University of California at Davis. There can be found pupils from all over the world learning first-hand the combined wisdom of wine making from past ages to the very latest, exacting discoveries on how to make better and better wine. Many of the students go back to their homelands of France, Germany, Switzerland, Greece, South Africa, and Australia with practical knowledge and experience that ordinarily would have taken a lifetime or two to acquire.

I'm told that watching grapevines grow and produce will never replace girl-watching, even though I can't be so sure of that after observing some of the characters who visited the vineyards and ogled the vines.

I assured one and all that it takes two years (sometimes only one) before the vines bear grapes but it is three or four years before they are usually picked because, until then, they are too immature for wine.

Vines take about twelve years before they are ready for top production. Depending on the type of grape, they yield about two to four tons per acre. (It takes two and one-half pounds of grapes to make a fifth of wine.) There are approximately 153 gallons per ton which gives us only about 765 bottles. This great length of growing time and small amount of tonnage per acre accounts for the worthwhile price fine table wines command.

It still amazes me how much good United States wine is sold at prices almost anyone can afford.

Before becoming a resident of California I'd been sampling the wines of that state whenever I could find them in the liquor stores. However, since, outside of European wines, the stores carried mainly New York state products, I was more familiar with the taste of wines from that grape-producing area. And, there is a difference. It's caused by the soil and climate.

In the United States, California has soil and climate similar to the traditionally held great grape-producing regions of Europe. Winters in most other places in the U.S. are too severe and there is not enough sun to bring to harvest a worthwhile table wine grape whose forebears were from European rootstock. The native American grape is much too sweet to be made into wine for drinking with the meal. Consequently, most table wines, outside of California's, come from hybrid vines: a mixture of European and those native to this country. (There are now proven geographical pockets in Washington and Oregon with the splendid soil and climate conditions essential for growing fine table wine varietals.)

To say that wines from one area of the United States are better than another is a matter of what taste one has gotten used to as well as having had experience with different types of wine. Trying out several kinds of wine once will not prove anything to anyone, except, perhaps, how much you can drink. The first comparison usually selects the customary taste and discards the unfamiliar. Only later tastings can crack the barrier.

As one master winemaker explained, "I was at a champagne tasting where five of the finest California brands, two French and two New York champagnes were sampled. Most of the people attending were from New York state. The bottles were covered so the labels could not be seen. The consensus was the two New York wines came in as the winners. Most of the tasters were used to the particular blends of grapes from their own regions and turned thumbs-down on the others."

The wine grapes from New York, Illinois, and Ohio have much in common. Most all are different from those grown in the table wine grape regions of northern California in that those of the other states have a stronger, more grapelike taste. You are well aware you are tasting a grape and most of them would make delectable table grapes if they weren't so expensive.

Some of the California table wine grapes are sweet enough to pick off the vine and pop into one's mouth but they are best used for wine as *le bon Dieu* intended them to be.

It sometimes seems that just about every winery classifies itself as "premium." It can't be blamed. The word is sort of all-embracing and, after all, the winery in question certainly doesn't want to say, "We're really second grade."

A general standard to remember is that the premium label on wines should mean the wines are of the highest quality and probably of the highest prices. But just because some wine from the United States costs $4.00 and another $2.00 per bottle does not mean that one is necessarily inferior to the other. You have to know the type of grape. One grape may be a bigger producer per acre; its price can then be lower. Even the same grape when handled in greater volume can lower the price. But when Cabernet Sauvignon in the fall of 1972 went for $900 per ton, you certainly aren't going to be able to buy that varietal wine for much less than $3.50 unless the winery has many acres of the grape.

Finally, some wines might not be of so-called premium quality; yet they may be very agreeable to the taste and to the wallet as well.

What's a varietal? Exactly what it implies: a certain variety of grape. Such as Pinot Noir, Cabernet Sauvignon, Pinot Chardonnay — these are the names of the grape and the wine. When you come to names such as Burgundy, Claret, and Rhine, they mean (in the U.S.) wine made from grapes with characteristics similar to the ones grown in those Old World regions.

Ed Norman, a salesman to the wineries who is also one of the most respected and loved people in the wine business, told me that so far the only way to successfully package wine is in bottles. Cans have been tried many times and I myself remember some few years ago getting a case of Beaujolais in cans. It wasn't bad. In fact, I was surprised it was so good. But then suddenly I couldn't find the wine any longer. Ed, the expert, says that a can is metal and even with a lacquer coating, wine will penetrate it, hit the metal, and the taste will be affected.

Another reason is that the public response to wine in cans is negative.

Almost any wine that has not had any fortification of alcohol (brandy added to bring up the alcohol content) will keep aging provided it has a cork. A premium wine that is less than fourteen percent alcohol (natural, nothing added) and from top-rated grapes would be bottled with a cork. The porous cork allows the wine, a living organism, to continue breathing. The finest wines are always corked. Lots of people prefer to keep them for years in a wine cellar and bring them out on special occasions. However, just because a wine bottle has a screw top by no means denotes junk. Many good wines that have not been aged long, and are made for the person who drinks *vino* daily but certainly cannot afford a dollar or two per day for his libation, are available for consumption at a price everyone can bear.

One definite point about wine: it is impossible to make fine wine from inferior grapes. The great wine grapes have been known for centuries and are absolutely necessary for wines of highest quality.

Many things can happen to spoil a good dry table wine after it has been bottled.

Remember: it should not be handled roughly; the bottle should be kept on its side. It is taken for granted that if it is a special wine it will have a cork, and the cork must be kept moist — otherwise it will dry out and then an air pocket will form and the wine will change chemically. But once the cork has been pulled, it is no longer necessary to keep the bottle on its side and the wine should be drunk within a day or two.

Should you have no wine on hand but need it for a party, try to purchase it a few days ahead and let it rest on its side in a cool place. Louie Benoist was so insistent on perfection that he would never drink a wine that someone had just delivered to him via a car, even if chauffeured. The reason: the poor little wine was shook up and needed to rest. 'Tis true: the wine does get disturbed when jostled around in a car or carried by hand a few blocks. However, few wine drinkers would realize the chemistry balance wasn't what it should be, so I certainly don't advocate switching to Scotch and water if the wine hasn't been allowed to relax for a few days after the purchase. If it's had a few hours to rest, go ahead and drink it.

A fine white wine should be aged from one to two years and a red from three to four before being released for sale.

The main reason many potentially excellent wines are sold before receiving the aging the winemaker would prefer is supply and demand. Due to the heavy market, in recent years the majority of the premium wineries all over the world are generally giving the minimum of aging to their wines and expecting the purchaser to appreciate a good buy and keep the wine around awhile to make it truly a gem for the palate.

Getting to know what's worthwhile and what's a good buy in European wines takes a lot of trials which uncork a lot of errors. Price alone does not denote a good bottle of wine. I've found that sometimes the quaint or different type of bottle the wine comes in is what should be kept and the wine poured out — down the sink. I don't feel too uncharitable in saying that lots of the inexpensive wines of Europe could be classified as "rotgut." I used to go around making the statement, somewhat apologetically, that fifty percent of all the wines from Europe weren't as good as the most inexpensive from California. I was taken to task by several top winemakers. Their criticism: not fifty percent of the wines from Europe, but seventy-five are not as good as California's least expensive!

The reason for this is that most European wines are produced without the companies having to adhere to such high standards as those set in the United States and particularly in California. Because the climate is so unstable, when ordering a wine from Europe one *must* know the year: was it a good, mediocre or bad vintage? Then it is necessary to know the vineyard.

In California the climate has few variations; there is seldom an extreme. One looks for the reliable labels and, for a beginner, the best way is to go by price. Later on you can decide which wines are as good for maybe fifty cents or even a dollar less per bottle.

It can be a lifetime game, albeit a cultural one, learning to appreciate wine.

The remarkable popularity of wine among the general public during the past twenty years can be attributed to several reasons: word-of-mouth publicity given to the merits of wine by the thousands of G.I.'s who have been stationed in Europe since World War II, the absolutely tremendous nationwide promoting job done by many wineries, neighbors sharing with others a bottle of wine they found delightful, and the general trend toward "lighter" alcoholic drinks.

Wine sales are upping in such states as Kentucky, Tennessee and Wyoming, none of these heretofore noted for wine consumption. And in Milwaukee today it is not just beer and the Brewers. Sales and advertising attest to the fact that wine has become very much of an "in" beverage.

As far as a natural promotion for wines, it's hard to beat a motel in Fresno, a major production area for California wines, that specializes in advertising wines as much as rooms.

The hostelry is Del Webb's TowneHouse, decorated entirely with a wine theme. The meeting rooms carry names such as the Burgundy Room, Moselle, Semillon. All the guest rooms are adorned in a wine motif — pictures of people picking grapes, scenes of vineyards. Naturally, the bar is called the Wine Press.

But I forgot to check whether the Gideon Bibles have the passages mentioning wine underlined!

CHAPTER IX

UNCORKING: WINE TIPS

Learning about wine is a fun thing. To start the study requires only a beginner's interest, a tongue that hasn't, during the previous few minutes, partaken of a lot of garlic, tobacco or Tabasco sauce. And when there is a wine tasting room or a wine tasting affair going on about town, there is very little need of spending money.

Whenever anyone asks: "Mary, how can I know what wines to drink and learn at least basic information about wine?" the best answer I can give is to suggest reading one or two elementary, easy-to-understand wine books, and, if at all possible, go to wine tasting rooms. If these are not available, attend any public wine tastings given in your city. Should the tasting rooms or the tastings open to the public be nonexistent, then I recommend getting together with three or four friends and each person buying two bottles of different kinds of wine and having your own private tasting. Keep this practice up every two weeks for six months (coupled with reading a book on wine every month) and you can consider yourself becoming a knowledgeable wine buff.

But visiting wine tasting rooms is the simplest, most comprehensive and educational method of learning the wine story.

If there are several wineries in the area you are really in luck. Each one should be visited two to three times within a period of a few weeks. In this way you can familiarize yourself with the wines. Also you should never taste more than eight at one visit. Even if you have only two or three sips of each, after five or six wines the taste buds just aren't as sharp as they should be in order to discover correctly one's preferences.

Say there are five wineries in your area. Aim for visiting two or three in one day. If two, try three or four wines at each. If three, have two or three wines at each. Then, a week or two later return to those tasting rooms for other wines. Be sure to keep a checklist of the ones you prefer. After visiting each of the five wineries two or three times, return and resample your favorite wines. You'll then be able to intelligently compare your choices of one winery with those of another.

This sampling takes a bit of time and planning but is the absolutely finest and most inexpensive manner of learning about wines and the various companies that make them.

For those who will visit a wine tasting room only when on a trip some distance from home, my advice is to read the description of the wines printed in the brochure available, decide on five or six to sample, take your time in sipping and even ask for a bit more of a repeat if there are one or two you're not sure of. But if you're truly interested in finding out about wines and which ones you might enjoy the most, I repeat, *don't* taste more than eight, maximum. And the trick to remember is that if you are going to taste more than three you should clear your palate (tongue) with a swallow or two of water between each wine, or have half of a cracker or a bite of French bread between samples.

Having been on both sides of the wine tasting bar, I know what the public wants, what the public is entitled to, and what the person pouring the wine expects from the public.

The public wants to taste as much wine as they can for free. This statement encompasses those who are primarily out for an afternoon of imbibing on the house with never a thought of buying and those, who, like you and I, wish to sample a limited amount of the winery's product so as to compare and eventually buy.

Most wineries consider the public entitled to taste as much as the house rule permits. Translated, this means that some wineries allow a person to taste everything they make while others will specify only certain wines. (There are also some wineries that are so crowded with visitors that only two or three wines are allowed the guests in order to keep the crowd moving.) With few exceptions, champagne is not served. This is because of the high taxes on the bubbly. Brandy is likewise not served for the same reason distilleries don't serve samples of bourbon or Scotch — high alcohol tax.

The host or hostess behind the tasting bar expects very little from the visitor. Merely simple courtesy. Spelled out this implies: no vulgar language, no glasses thrown, no wine thrown, no insulting the product and no great expectations of getting personalized service when there are seventeen other people at the bar and two people serving.

Must you buy after sampling a few drinks?

No. And, as long as you haven't made a bore or otherwise nuisance of yourself, feel free to come back, even if the personnel remembers you. It doesn't hurt to say "thank you" for the tasting and for the time spent trying to convince you that that company's wine is superior to others. And, I would highly suggest that if you think enough of the wines to return the third time, and believe you will be recognized, purchase a bottle before starting the tasting. If not recognized, it certainly would be nice, if for no other reason than conscience, to buy a bottle when leaving. Who knows? You might want to come back again. And the climate will at least seem more hospitable if you act appreciative.

There are over two hundred wineries in California, most of them located in the northern part of the state. Through the years I have been to about three-quarters of the larger, better-known tasting rooms. And to many of the smaller, not so well-known ones. Like everyone, I have preferences. And, likewise, my preferences differ from those of others.

The wine tasting rooms I shall discuss in this chapter are some I have found particularly interesting. Most of them are well known to the public, some only to the seeker-out of yet another fine wine. As I mentioned before, all wineries give special tours and treatment to retailers, distributors, and other VIPs who can benefit them in large-scale selling. Some of the wineries have facilities for the general public's use for picnics, luncheons, private tastings, etc. I shall note only facilities open to the general public.

To start on a sad, negative reminder: "my" winery, Almadén, now has a "No Visitors" sign outside the front gates. The winery plant has become so around-the-clock busy that it is a hazard to have visitors walk through. "My" cottage is now used for meetings of department heads while the winemaster uses "my" private little tasting room for sampling with other VIPs in the wine industry.

A few miles away, though, in Saratoga, the visitor to Paul Masson Winery can't help but be awed at the modern plant itself and contented with the welcoming committee. It used to be a challenge to me whenever I had visitors who were going to both Almadén and Paul Masson the same day. Although friendly, we were very competitive.

Many visitors asked how both Almadén and Masson could claim the same birth date: 1852. Well, Paul Masson was a son-in-law of the founder of Almadén. He eventually started his own vineyard and carried on with the date.

Except for the usual holidays, Masson's is open every day of the year. They will serve forty of their wines but not Blanc de Pinot champagne or brandy.

Catching a glimpse of Wally Raich, Sr., the Director of Hospitality, is almost worth the visit to the winery. Wally, with his European-style walrus moustache and his refined and gracious manner, can be seen explaining to special guests the workings of the winery, making suggestions that they taste such and such. I must admit that Masson has some of the easiest-to-get-along-with tasting room hosts I've ever encountered. Tasting there can be fun as well as educational. Children are even made "at home" by being given a sucker and a coloring book!

Paul Masson has continuous tours of the winery. It also has facilities for private, catered luncheons and dinners or by-reservation, do-your-own barbeques.

Just one mile up in the hills from downtown Los Gatos is

the Novitiate Winery and tasting room. Owned and operated by the Jesuit priests and brothers, this winery is a gem of a find for the wine buff. It could be a small gold mine for the Jesuits if they operated it properly. Like the stories about the Army assigning a person who had been a cook in private life to work in the library or a librarian to work in the maintenance department, so goeth the good padres at the Novitiate.

I keep telling myself that it must be the grace of God and also winemaker Brother Lee Williams's talent that keeps putting out wines as good as theirs are. They have several table wines that are excellent and some of their dessert wines are marvelous. Their Black Muscat cannot be beat as a heavy dessert wine tasting almost exactly like the grape. I preferred their ports to Almadén's and we'd do an exchange. Their Flor Sherry is another favorite of mine.

Once in Los Gatos, it's easy to find their winery. The tour, given by a black-robed brother, is something special. The wine tasting room, right in the cellars with huge redwood casks about, is pleasing. The tasting bar is oak from the flight deck of an aircraft carrier. Children are welcomed and given soda pop while the adults go about eating bread sticks and tasting the eighteen wines available. This is one of the rare wineries in California where it is possible to watch the "crush" of the grapes taking place right on the grounds.

Catered luncheons and private wine tastings by appointment. By all means, Novitiate is a "must" for the discerning winery visitor.

A small winery in Los Gatos of special interest to me is that of David Bruce. Tours of the winery and tastings are by appointment. David Bruce wines command some of the highest prices I've ever seen posted. I hear they are quite good. I've never bought any — not at those prices.

This winery is special, though, as far as I'm concerned, because it is owned by my dermatologist, David Bruce. He wears the most atrocious unmatched sock and tie combinations I've ever come across. However, I can attest to the fact that he knows how to cure strange looking blotches on one's face as well as how to lecture that a woman should never wear makeup. (David, not all men go for that natural, well-scrubbed look!)

A vineyard fast, fast coming into the limelight as a producer of quality wines as well as hospitality *par excellence* is Mirassou Vineyards in San Jose.

Although this family has been making wines in Santa Clara County for the past one hundred years, until recently it has produced mainly wines in bulk quantities for other wineries besides selling them grapes. Then, about seven years ago the fifth generation of Mirassous decided they should bottle with their own label. What a touch of enthusiasm and freshness they've given the wine market! Mirassou wines are now beginning to be sold nationwide. But, since they are trying to keep to the quality standard, there will be a limited supply for some time. Steve and Peter and Dan Mirassou are proving to their respective fathers, Norbert and Ed, that they too have the savvy needed to run a successful winery.

The tasting room has been open about five years. To see it in operation is to witness hospitality mixed with salesmanship unsurpassed. There must be some people who leave without buying cases, not bottles. But the person who just drops by is given such an unforgettable time that you'd really have to be completely broke or terribly insensitive not to want to buy the place out!

Besides tasting wines in balloon-sized glasses, one may reserve a date for a catered luncheon. (If you're one of the special VIPs, the Mirassou family will let you either shoot your own quail on their premises or they will both shoot it and dress it for your dinner. Naturally, wines are included.)

One tasting room (no winery tours) to visit if you're in the vicinity is San Martin. There are five in northern California with the main one located on Highway 101 in San Martin, about thirty minutes from San Jose heading south toward Carmel. Each of the rooms has a slightly different style. All display a unique way of getting the public to know and enjoy their wines. And there are foods to buy and all sorts of other gifts ranging from corkscrews to glasses to aprons to liqueur sets to candy. All San Martin tasting rooms are run in a gracious manner.

Besides table wines, they make some of the best possible natural fruit and berry wines.

About a half hour's drive from San Jose and a few miles east of San Francisco are the Livermore Valley wineries. Most of the visits I made to that area were to look at rare birds (winged kind) and to purchase them for our estate from Lee Poisal. Weibel Vineyards at the Mission San Jose has a lovely tasting room, and the surroundings are relaxing. If you're a person who enjoys strolling through cemeteries that bespeak history, then you'll love Mission San Jose, nearby the winery.

Weibel sells much of their champagnes to other wineries. The tip-off will be on the label: Bottled at Mission San Jose.

I wanted to see Concannon Vineyards because they produce a large amount of sacramental wine (for use in saying Mass). This winery tour and tasting is friendly, informal and typical of a small winery. Concannon also makes fine commercial wines for sale at retail stores.

In the commercials, one hears of Napa-Sonoma-Mendocino wines. Most visitors go to the Napa area. There are so many wineries in a close-by radius.

One of the best-known quality wineries in the Napa region is Beaulieu Vineyards, now owned by Heublein. (Wisely, the parent company allows it to be operated independently.) Going north from San Francisco, it and Louis Martini Winery are the first two one sees on the right-hand side. Beaulieu has a good tour and it is another fine example of a small, select winery.

Nearby Louis Martini Winery is noted for its excellent red wines. They give a highly informative tour, and extend a welcome to the new tasting room facilities.

The famed Christian Brothers Wine and Champagne Cellars look terribly impressive. Although much too sunny looking to conjure up visions of Dracula's Castle, castle it is. However, the tour itself is rather disappointing for most people — other than those strictly interested in getting to the tasting. Usually there is a torrent of visitors and this means being crowded into a small elevator and going into upstairs rooms where one is allowed to briefly glance at cases housing Brother Timothy's corkscrew collection and then seeing some tanks containing champagne. Then back down to the tasting area where, hopefully, you aren't in with a crowd of more than two dozen people. The bar can get awfully filled, and trying to obtain that third or fourth sample of wine proves you've got stamina. (Happily, their new touring and tasting facilities will be ready in 1974.)

Christian Brothers' salesmen do a lot of public relations work by pouring the wine at numerous private and public wine tastings throughout the U.S.A.

One minute's drive up the road is Beringer Winery. Beringer has always been one of my three top choices for visiting in California if you want to see atmosphere and what you think a winery should look like. The winery aging section is limestone caves which certainly lends itself to a bygone day. The caves are very cool and one can visualize men digging them out in order to insure the proper temperature for the wines.

Beringer's red-coated hosts welcome everyone and give the tours. If it is possible to go other than during the summer and fall tourist season, it should be done in order to taste several wines. Should you arrive when scads of people are about, you will be taken, out of necessity, to the tasting room and given two wines (of the day) and then out to allow another group to come in. Facilities are available for private parties by appointment. The former library of the Beringer family chateau is now the tasting room for VIPs.

The champagne house to watch nowadays is Schramsberg Vineyards (tours by appointment only). Some connoisseurs think they produce the finest champagne in the U.S. The Schramsberg name was first heard worldwide by most when TV newscasters mentioned it was the champagne served at the dinner President Nixon hosted when visiting Peking. I was told that it was the Pinot Chardonnay grapes that Beringer sold Schramsberg that went into the making of this historic beverage. Schramsberg's Blanc de Blancs champagne was also chosen for President Nixon's banquet in Moscow.

At the southernmost end of the winery strip in Napa County is Robert Mondavi Winery. Bob Mondavi, a breakaway from his family-owned Krug Winery, started his Mondavi Winery with his son Mike in 1966 and by 1967 wine was being sold. This winery has become so well known already that they are booked months in advance for catered lunches and dinners. Also, every six weeks there is an exhibit of a different artist's works. So many artists find showing at Mondavi profitable (the winery takes a ten percent commission) and alluring that the exhibit gallery is booked through two years in advance!

Rarely do wineries bottle in magnums as well as fifths and tenths; Mondavi does. I find this winery one of the most attractive I have ever seen. The view of the vineyards is magnificent and the architect who designed the Spanish mission-style winery and other buildings did a superb job. It's pretty difficult to emulate the original missions. Most often it comes out like a Hollywood set, rather than an authentic copy. Mondavi comes across as an original. The views through the archways simply have to be designed by nature. A must-see winery, even if you're not invited by Bob or Mike to taste special wines set up on a little table right smack in the vineyards.

There is such a multitude of wineries in Napa County, and they have publicized themselves so highly during the past thirty-five years, that all you have to do is mention wine from California and practically everyone thinks of Napa. Well, the truth of the matter is that there are other fine wine-producing regions and right next door to Napa is one of them — Sonoma.

The city of Sonoma might as well be called the city of Sebastiani because the Sebastianis, who own and operate the winery, are considered by many to be immensely responsible for the city's prosperity and growth since grandfather Samuele came to this part of the world from Italy. He purchased the winery in 1904.

By merely taking a quick look at the center of town — the plaza, church, restaurants and shops around the plaza — and then seeing the winery, one can figure out what the town must have looked like at the turn of the century. Anyway, the Sebastianis moved in and they have been making history since.

I love Sonoma and the Sebastianis but I'm still enough of a reporter and expert at sizing up wineries to make an honest appraisal and, therefore, enthusiastically endorse a visit to this truly historic spot.

The tasting room and cellars are open daily; the employees know what they are talking about and they have a small-town friendliness. When there, you get a touch of early California days, even though the name of the winery isn't Spanish.

Possibly the most famous name winery in California is

Haraszthy Cellars-Buena Vista Winery in Sonoma. Its founder, Count Agoston Haraszthy, was the first person to import European varietal cuttings on a large scale for planting in California. He is considered by many to be the "father" of California's modern-day wine and grape industry.

The original cellars, dug out of limestone, are still in use. This is the only winery I know of where the visitor gives himself a tour. It is delightful exploring the winding caves to the tasting room grotto.

For the travel weary, the perfect windup is to purchase, while in the tasting room, a snack of bread and cheese, a chilled bottle of Haraszthy's famed Green Hungarian and then loll in the tree-shaded vistas of the winery grounds.

About an hour out of San Francisco, north on Highway 101, you'll spot signs advertising wineries that are right off the freeway. There are a dozen such wineries within ten or twelve minutes' driving distance apart.

A bit past Santa Rosa is Windsor Vineyards and Winery. One of the two architectural structures that I find esthetically disturbing, it, nonetheless, houses a unique establishment. (Having been bred wine-wise in an atmosphere of caves, tunnels, and rows and rows of barrels, the futuristic, almost Disneyland look of Paul Masson always gave me a shock. Of course, the more I saw Masson's main winery, the less upset I was. Maybe this will happen with Windsor.)

As it now seems to me, it is a very late twentieth-century redwood edifice reminding me of a Miami Beach motel, an office housing a complex of architects, or a nondenominational church trying to appeal to the masses.

Lots of people love the place. I like the people who people it.

Windsor Winery provides a tasting room with tables and chairs for leisurely sipping, a lot of ground for people to picnic on, rooms in which to partake of catered meals and even a gourmet cook, a lovely woman who is now giving lessons in French cooking. She will prepare, by appointment, a special meal. Wines, of course, may be had with the meal. Some fancy restaurants may allow the guests to rent their wine cellar, but not many people get the opportunity to actually dine, surrounded by barrels, *in* the wine cellar of a winery! Windsor's the word.

If it's champagne cellars you'd like to see, do go to Korbel. Located in Guerneville, in Sonoma County, for almost a century it has been noted for its superb champagnes. Although, since the mid 1950s, no longer in the hands of the Korbel family, this winery continues to turn out a remarkable champagne and is now concentrating on the still wine market as well.

There is always a champagne the visitor may taste and sometimes two or three. The tasting room is somewhat reminiscent of what you'd expect of a first-rate saloon in the West of the 1870s, '80s and '90s. Massive bar, red velvet spilled around, crystal chandeliers, thick carpeting. No ordinary saloon, for sure. Be certain, when visiting Korbel, to allow an extra five or ten minutes to just stand outside, enjoy the scenery of the Russian River area, and inhale the smog-free oxygen. (And, if you want to see two of today's finest young wine-making breed, ask and maybe you'll catch a glimpse of Alan Hemphill, the winemaker, and Jimmy Huntsinger, his assistant. The latter is the son of Almadén's winemaster.)

Twenty minutes north of Santa Rosa, off 101 and on the Old Redwood Highway, nestling right into the hillside, out of which the winery was hewed back in 1876, is Simi Winery. Founded by one of those industrious Italians who helped make Sonoma County one of the greatest agricultural areas of the U.S., Giuseppi Simi, along with his brother, Pietro, decided that this section of the world so resembled their native Montepulciano, Italy, that a winery should be built commemorating this discovery.

Until the past two years the tasting room was tiny, although cozy, and had a sort of "why don't you sit on a wine keg, pet the cat and sip a glass of red wine" atmosphere. Now, in a new building, the tasting area is larger. However, grey-haired, beautiful Mrs. Isabelle Simi Haigh (only daughter of Giuseppi) still rules the room and is the matriarch of the winery, even though she sold back in 1970. Another lovely person to reckon with is Mary Ann Graf, perhaps the nation's first female professional winemaker.

Simi is one of the few wineries to have an honest-to-goodness choo-choo train (courtesy, Northwestern Pacific) running right in front of its doors. While touring the cellars one should note the decades-old wall telephones, all of which are even now used as intercommunications systems.

Catered luncheons and dinners are available, as well as private tastings. There are also two areas of redwoods for picnickers.

Nearby Simi is a typical "mom and pop" operated winery, which means it is run exclusively by the family. Nervo Winery is the name. Almost one hundred years old, the tasting room will allow you to sample any of the products, except champagne bought from Korbel. Since the Nervos are always busy pruning the vines, picking the grapes, fermenting the juice, seeing the wine is aged properly, bottling the wine, labeling and running the tasting room, sometimes the stock is limited. Much of their wine is sold to large producers such as Gallo. Nervo makes a Pinot St. George that is unusual. Buying their jug wine, in half gallons or gallons, is one of the best economic moves a wine appreciator can make.

A very small winery with a tiny tasting room, it nonetheless gives a true picture and flavor of many wineries in California. Frank Nervo, in coveralls, will probably wait on you and, if you're lucky enough to engage him in conversation, there is a wealth of wine information he can pour forth. It's people like him who have kept the vineyards through good and bad times, who weathered the Prohibition era and who furnish character and color to the wine industry.

I used to inwardly seethe (and often show it) when visitors to Almadén, thinking they were being complimentary, would make a remark like, "Well, boy, this sure isn't Gallo," or "I bet you'd hate to work at some place like Italian Swiss Colony that really pushes out the stuff."

Both of the wineries mentioned make good wine. And all of their wine is better than most from Europe thrice as expensive. Best of all, people who drink wine every day can afford their tasty product. I know what I'm talking about; the positive proof being I've even paid full price for both of these brands!

As a place to visit, Italian Swiss Colony at Asti can't be beat. The northernmost end of Sonoma County, just off 101, you see the original grounds of "The Little Old Winemaker." I expected him to appear.

There is an area for picnickers. The tasting rooms are bubbling with fermented juices of the grapes and the personalities of the wine pourers and tour guides. Everything is so beautifully arranged and organized, I would classify this as a top spot for families to stop. Children are welcomed. There are free post cards to mail, cookies for everyone, and even big cardboard cutouts of Swiss-costumed men and women minus heads that you can be photographed behind — with your own head showing. The whole setup is arranged for your convenience, your comfort, and for serious wine drinkers it's a surprise bonanza! I curtsy to the Rossis, Joe Vercelli and Heublein's for Italian Swiss Colony.

In Mendocino do stop by Parducci if you've got a half-hour minimum. You're in for a treat. Especially if Margaret Parducci is able to show you through. The winery has been in operation since 1932 and, although small, it's not microscopic. Margaret hears every visitor. She has a bell rigged to her house that clangs whenever anything rides, steps, glides or slithers over a spot directly in the roadway. No manner of avoiding it. The door handles to the winery are massive corkscrews made by John Parducci. The winery itself is spic and span, one of the cleanest I've ever seen. (Maybe Margaret does go around daily with scrub brush and pail.) The tasting room was formerly the Parducci family wine cellar.

It's the wines that are the surprise. I'd heard how good they were but paid very little heed. How taken aback I was when trying them. There are about twenty-four in all, quite a number for a medium-small winery. The quality is what completely amazes me. I will not state that I personally consider them the finest I have tasted in the United States, but I will emphatically say that I seldom have tasted so many of such a superior quality from any winery.

Parducci's is one winery I am hoping to visit again and I pray such wines as theirs will continue on into the next and the next and the next generation.

Before purchasing wine, there are four questions you should ask yourself:

1) When am I going to use the wine? With the meal? Before the meal? After the meal?

2) How much can I afford to pay?

3) What would I *really* like to buy? (My advice: unless it's terribly far out, get it!)

4) Will I use enough to buy the "economy" size of a half gallon or gallon? (Only a savings if used within a week after opening.)

Aside from dozens of pamphlets put out by various wineries, there are four books I would recommend as easy reading and loaded with information. These books are for the person willing to spend several hours absorbing each book. I've read over a hundred books on wine, but, all in all, if you read a select few you can have a fair knowledge of what you're talking about and then go on to delve more deeply into the subject matter.

Still my basic favorites:

The Complete Wine Book by Frank Schoonmaker and Tom Marvel; Simon and Schuster, New York (hopefully, someplace besides a library has a copy).

Wines by Julian Street; Alfred A. Knopf, New York.

Guide to California Wines by John Melville; Nourse Publishing Company, San Carlos, California.

A History of Wine by H. Warner Allen; Faber and Faber, London, England.

HAPPY READING AND SIPPING!

CHAPTER X

KICK THE WINE SNOB HABIT

Wine snobs are bores. And I've noticed this type of bore is becoming commonplace.

No one is born a wine snob, but it is very easy to fall into this habit. It takes a broad-minded, intelligent person to avoid the pitfall.

When an adult first decides to learn about wine, he is usually eager, listens to those with more knowledge of the subject and generally keeps his mouth shut except to ask an occasional, more likely than not, stupid question. The beginner, because he is sincerely seeking information, can be patiently tolerated. So, all is happiness at first between student and instructor. Then, like the proverbial college sophomore, the wine snob thinks he knows it all. Even worse, unlike the sophomore, who goes through a year of being a freshman, the Mr. Wine-Know-It-All has but to read three books on wine, several brochures, visit a few wineries, sample some wines and we have an instant expert.

Wine snobs fool nobody but those who know as little about wine as the snob.

The true wine buff or connoisseur follows one cardinal rule: he does not *act* like he knows it all. (If you *think* you do, keep it to yourself.)

Some of the greatest all-around winemakers in the United

States, men such as Louie M. Martini, Brad Webb, Myron Nightingale, Roy Mineau and Leonard Berg, are walking storehouses of wine know-how. Yet, each is a perfect example of a nonsnob. If asked a question, of course they will answer it. Should it be a technical, scientific matter, they will factually reply just as anyone knowing two and two add up to four will answer with certainty. But, ask them or any other top expert which red wine is the best in the world or who produces the finest champagne and none will give an answer other than their personal opinion. They adhere to the old saying: *De gustibus non disputandis*. (Freely translated: no quarrel over tastes.)

When wine experts are professionally tasting wines, they make remarks such as "heavy in volatile acid," "too much sulphur." But in a normal conversation, technical speech is seldom used. They expect the other person to be aware of what is and isn't wrong with the wine and they don't count on the nonprofessional knowing all the terminology. Hence, no showing off.

Don't talk too much to show what you don't know. Unless expressing a scientific fact, preface your remarks with "well, my opinion would be" or "I personally have found," etc. You will be appreciated, looked upon as an intelligent person, and maybe even liked.

Times are changing for the better for the customer buying wine at liquor stores, grog shops, and wine shops. Until about the mid 1960s, unless you were lucky enough to live in an area where a lot of wine was sold, finding a store where the salesclerks or even the owner-manager knew anything about wine other than the prices was difficult.

Today, in almost every large city there is some shop where wines are featured and the customer can rely on the salesperson having a knowledge of wine.

I've been fortunate in having met some modern day "pioneers" in wine retail sales. Each time I encountered one of these esteemed people, my life would be brightened. It would help make up for the dozens of retailers who'd been stocking wines for years but never bothered to learn anything about them and, consequently, couldn't promote or sell them successfully. Many times, in years past, I had asked the salesmen's advice about a wine and, instead of their frankly saying they didn't know much about wines, they would bluff or make up some story. Invariably I would find out the truth and wonder about the salesmen.

I entertained many wine retail sales people who had such belief in the beverage and its future that they began actively promoting it years ahead of others.

One person who had such foresight is John Beltramo. Although still in law school in 1963, John intended to help carry on his father's package store business. The oldest liquor store on the Peninsula of northern California, Beltramo's in Menlo Park sells only products they know about. All of the Beltramos are wine connoisseurs and the people they employ must likewise be cognizant of what they are talking about. Alex, John's father, once recounted to me his feelings about certain homemade wines and I still giggle at the memory.

I had told Alex that I imagined he, being Italian, made some great wines. I certainly didn't expect his answer. In rather colorful language he assured me he did not make his own wines, there were such superior wines on the market, even some inexpensive ones, that making one's own was a lot of unnecessary bother. Furthermore, said he, whenever he was invited to the home of one of his old Italian friends and he knew they served their own made wines, he, Alex, always brought at least two bottles of something from his own store. He wasn't going to drink anything tasting like it had been aged in chicken coop wire!

Besides being totally familiar with wines of the U.S., every year or so the Beltramos tour the vineyards and wineries throughout Europe in order to learn even more to pass on to the customer.

Another boon to the industry is Ed Younger, the wine consultant for the Johnathan Club in Los Angeles, who knows just about every good buy of American and European wines. Besides that, he is professionally capable of tasting along with the best of the winemakers. Although still a young man, Ed has had twenty years of experience in the wine field and admits he'll always be searching for more information.

The father of noted wine writer Robert Lawrence Balzer started a trend, in southern California, for markets heavily promoting wines. Bob's father owned one of the most exclusive and fantastic gourmet shops ever in business. This was until about World War II when he sold to Jurgensen's. There probably are no more places such as his. Not enough call for fresh Iranian Beluga caviar, specially raised snails, *pâte' de foie*, cans of truffles and other such expensive trifles. Being able to taste and enjoy every item in that shop, I'm sure, influenced Bob into becoming a superb wine and food expert.

Recently, many chain stores, with wide-awake management, have started "gourmet" sections. These stores can afford to hope for good sales in that area without depending solely on it. However, within the past few years, they have found the department is paying off handsomely; so, accordingly, more and more buyers and managers are touring vineyards and tasting rooms and putting their newly found wine knowledge to work for them, the company, and the customer.

Although in business only about ten years, both Pronto Markets and their other gourmet stores, Trader Joe's, are the envy of many firms who have been around for triple that time. It's a young company in all ways: the age of the average executive and the bright, fresh ideas always popping up. (They've even started a wine cellar where the customer, for a rental fee, can store his wine; naturally, the wine should be bought at Trader Joe's.)

Since I'd entertained several of their top management and was familiar with the business sharpness of their executives, I was upset when two unexpectedly showed at my doorstep.

It was early in January and I was trying to get in at least three or four days out of a supposed week's vacation. I had just returned from having a plaster cast sawed off my left leg and hobbled, via crutches, up the porch steps and into the house when a call came from the winery office: "Two men from Trader Joe's to see you and be shown around."

Had the San Francisco office remembered to inform me they were coming, I would have arranged for someone else to take them about. Instead, I hurriedly found out there now was no one available at the winery. Though I wasn't officially at work, I hated to see the company put in an embarrassing situation so I said, "Send them over," all the while wondering if I needed fresh lipstick or a hair combing. Then as I hopped to the door to welcome them, I glanced down at my newly uncovered leg. It not only looked terribly thin but oh, horror: it was unshaven!

Greeting Leroy Watson and Frank Kono was a bit of a strain. I couldn't stop thinking about the five-week growth on my leg. Finally, the feminine me took over and I explained, "I just came out of a cast and if I'd known you were coming I'd have shaved!"

They put me at my ease, remarking there were only about five wineries they really enjoyed visiting and Almadén was one. They were even sweet enough to fetch the wine they wished to sample from the icebox. Then, since on this visit they were primarily interested in tasting and seeing the famous Solera Sherry cellars, they followed my instructions on winery routing and gave their own tour. Leroy and Frank were contented with the visit; I was happy they were happy.

I could understand that California retailers and restaurant owners would be aware of potential wine sales. But to find numbers of forward-thinking, wine-oriented people in states like New Jersey, Ohio, Illinois, Texas, Nevada and Minnesota was quite an eyeopener.

I'll always be grateful to Almadén's John Lemma for introducing me to dozens of folks engaged in promoting wines. One couple, Vern and Katy Anderson of Portland, Oregon, have a very fine and busy delicatessen called *Ideal* which features wine and cheese. Until I met the Andersons I'd never gone in for cheeses unless someone plain old set a plate in front of me and it would be impolite to refuse. Vern and Katy made me aware of just how complementary wine and cheese can be.

Over in Cambridge, Massachusetts, at the Oxford Grill, wine has been in ever since Anthony Pompeo and Albert DeVincentis became partners. And, according to the prices on the menu, even the scholarship students at Harvard can afford *vino*.

In New Jersey, head for Welsh's in Lambertville. They must sell, like they advertise, "fine wines and liquors" because no other owners show greater concern for their clientele than the Welshs — father and son. After two or three different visits to the winery, they made several long distance calls asking me for advice on various wines; what would go best for an Indian meal or at the reception following a Jewish wedding, as well as questions on handling wine, proper corking and on and on. In pushing wine, the Welshs, along with some other New Jersey stores, were years ahead of most of their so-called "big" competition in New York City.

A woman visitor in the wine business was so scarce that I immediately felt empathy and warmth toward her. So I was happy to greet Marjorie Valvano, manager of the Wine Cellar at the H. & S. Pogue Co. in Cincinnati, Ohio. Pogue's insists on only top-rate people in their store. (This might mean customers as well as employees!)

Well, Marjorie certainly fits the bill. Tall, brunette, glamorous, she knows her wines. Almost every year she is sent, by her employer, for three or four weeks to some wine-growing area: Europe one year, California the next, New York and then to Europe again and so on. This, of course, is invaluable toward her selling in the shop and buying the proper stock. All her work has paid off handsomely. She is well known throughout the wine world and respected as well.

I still marvel at meeting scads of wine-wise retailers from Minnesota. Like New Yorkers who think there is nothing going on outside of Manhattan, I had been in the habit of thinking of Minnesota as the land of lakes and lots of snow and ice.

Then I met Joanne and Bob Grimes who own Jennings Liquors in Minneapolis. A wine-conscious pair, both do a lot of travelling all over the wine-producing areas of the world and their customers line up to hear the latest wine story. Bob also writes a newspaper column on wine.

They agreed with me as to which clerks in grog shops to avoid: the ones who, even though not busy, act indifferent; those who immediately start a spiel about this or that imported wine being superior; those, who after giving you a lengthy glance, lead you to the least expensive American wines.

At least in a wine shop you can always mumble, "I was just looking," and walk away. But, in a restaurant, when the wine steward is annoying and unhelpful, the only way out is a fast, "sorry, no wine for us tonight."

I've been drinking wine in restaurants since early teen days and wasn't aware, until my first visit to New York City at nineteen, that there was an age law for being served alcoholic beverages. Evidently the law was not strictly enforced in New Orleans.

By the time I found myself professionally in the wine business, I'd become a bit blasé at seeing the wine steward striding around with tiny wine cup swinging on a lengthy chain about his neck.

Of course, back in my New Orleans' days I never dared question him. And, to this day I won't, but for different reasons. It's bad enough that most of my escorts hand *me* the wine list and expect me to order, and it's likewise a bit unnerving to have the sommelier surreptitiously stare at both of us. But the idea of my criticizing the wine to the sommelier is enough to cause embarrassment just thinking about it. I'll always believe it's a man's world and there are times when even I know when to keep quiet.

Today, more and more prominent restaurants are sending their people to schools and training sessions to learn about wine. Therefore, if some employee is an expert on European wines, they soon become knowledgeable about those from the United States and vice versa. Even smaller restaurants are promoting wines and finding they have a ready market. The managers of these spots are quick to discover it pays to give their dining room employees a course in wine appreciation and that the employees often go on their own time to various wineries with lists of questions they've already been asked by customers. I believe that, given a few more years, the average restaurant employee in the U.S. will know more about wines in general than their European counterparts.

And, just in case someone you know pretends to a total knowledge about wines, or, possibly, you believe you're getting a bit snobbish, I suggest reading four books that should produce humbleness even in an arrogant wine snob.

They are: *The Wines of America*, Leon D. Adams, San Francisco Book Company/Houghton Mifflin Company, Boston; *Wine, An Introduction for Americans*, M. A. Amerine and V. L. Singleton, University of California Press, Berkeley and Los Angeles; *Frank Schoonmaker's Encyclopedia of Wines*, Hastings House, New York; and *Wine and Your Well-Being*, Salvatore Pablo Lucia, M.D., Popular Library, New York.

CHAPTER XI

SOME FABULOUS PERSONAGES IN THE WINE INDUSTRY

I have discovered so many fantastic people in the wine industry in California, it does make the going a bit difficult in having to pick out only a very few for a capsule profile.

There are those behind-the-scenes giants; there are those winemakers, winery executives and notable personalities who are actively connected with the wine industry; and there are those, unknown to the general public, members of the news and public relations media who have made it their life's career in letting others be aware that "a day without wine is a day without sunshine."

I have met neither Ernest nor Julio Gallo. In fact, for some time I thought they were husband and wife; finally my nearsighted eyes detected that the Julio had an "o" and not an "a" as the last letter in the name. Well, at least I had always been aware that the team was one of the prime movers of the California wine business.

As is the case of anyone wielding tremendous power, Ernie Gallo is very controversial. But, whether disliked or admired, I have never heard him spoken of other than in a respectful tone. He is a genius in the wine industry and everyone with knowledge in that field is aware of this fact.

Both Ernest and Julio are kingpins of commercial wines, accounting for just a fraction below fifty percent of all the wines produced in California. Their headquarters building in Modesto has been dubbed "Parthenon West" by everyone but the public-shy Gallos. The caliber of executives like Charles Crawford, George Thoukis and Hector Castro is another proof why the Gallos maintain a thriving empire.

In the California wine trade there is one man who is a walking encyclopedia, a storehouse of personal knowledge, a confessor and a humanitarian; his name is Lou Gomberg.

A wine consultant and lawyer, Lou has been intimately associated with wineries per se since the 1930s. Few people have more of an overall picture of the wine industry in the United States than Lou.

If Lou was only out for money, by this time he would be a multimillionaire. He has helped many firms to locate the goose that lays the golden egg. At times he has even come out with a sizable purse but, somehow, it seems to go into a charitable cause. Lou would remake the world as many of us would be inclined to do. Only Lou does something about it besides hope.

Lou was the "go-between" in the Heublein takeover of United Vintners and Beaulieu. He is an expert at knowing what the present owner is seeking as a buyer and what the potential buyer wants. He gets them together with brotherly love. Lou is a wonderful human being.

The usual reaction when I mention Dr. Salvatore Lucia is, "What? That doc who raves about wine as if it were the only alcoholic beverage in the world?"

That's just why Salvatore Lucia is such a wine celebrity. He is the author of eight books and the spirit-emeritus of a group of physicians who have, for the past four years, held an international symposium singing the health benefits of wine.

Dr. Lucia has been on the faculty of the Medical School of the University of California, San Francisco, since 1931. He is former chairman of the Department of Preventive Medicine and has held full professorships in both Medicine and Preventive Medicine. He is very serious on important matters. In general conversation he is so convincing a wine advocate that many innocents could be swayed into believing maybe a three-ounce glass of wine would be of benefit to their corns!

A powerful man behind the scenes, widely recognized because of his being in the wine business for three decades plus, is Leon Adams. Author of seventeen wine books, twelve of which he "ghosted" for others, he has just had his latest manuscript, *The Wines of America*, published. Leon's *The Commonsense Book of Wine*, written years ago, is rated a classic.

Leon co-founded and helped steer the California Wine Institute through its formative years and, mainly because of a few men like him, the Institute is now so successful. Leon Adams is still personally very active in telling the wine story and generously giving others the benefit of his perception and know-how in the wine field.

Two professors who could equally and rightfully be called "Mr. Know-It-All" of the wine world are Maynard Amerine and Harold Berg, both of the University of California at Davis.

Dr. Amerine is known and honored worldwide for his technical writings and information on wine. He has had his own TV show explaining the wine story and, aside from being called a wine connoisseur with an *A+* rating, he maintains a good enough sense of humor to smile when someone notes his holding a glass containing a martini.

Hal Berg's name keeps coming up when wine people tell tall tales about other wine people. Professor Berg, whose brother, Leonard Berg, is considered one of the greatest winemakers in the nation, is Chairman of the Enology and Viticulture Department at Davis. The first time I spoke with him at any length was via telephone asking advice on a serious professional matter.

Since I'd met the man only twice, both times briefly, and as I was new in the business, I didn't know how he would take to this request. I shouldn't have worried. He treated me as a colleague, taking it for granted I would keep secret the intelligence source. I respected him and his consideration of me and ever since then I have been a fan of Hal Berg.

Handling dual roles of background strength and influential newsmen in the forefront are Irving Marcus and Phil Hiaring.

Irving was for years both editor and publisher of the monthly magazine *Wines & Vines*, the authoritative voice of the wine industry. He is presently devoting most of his sixteen-hour day trying to meet requests for wine articles from various periodicals. His recent book, *Lines about Wines*, is a collection of editorials he wrote over the past thirty years.

Irving is kind and gentle and always remembers your name, and I prefer to believe that he really does recall and hasn't just asked someone else your identity before addressing you. He is one of the grand older men of the wine industry.

It is red-headed, freckle-faced Phil Hiaring who has exuberantly and competently taken over the publishing of *Wines & Vines*. Although years younger, Phil has had almost as much firsthand know-how about the wine scene as Irving. He's a columnist, lecturer, Full Colonel in the Air Force Reserve, and a *bon vivant*.

I had been at Almadén but a few months when Phil came for a tour and tasting at the winery with a group of his public relations friends from San Francisco. Phil wrote up the Almadén affair most favorably and gave a heretofore unknown winery hostess a big boost. My "notoriety" had started.

Phil is a top reporter: objective, fair, a listener and a keeper of confidences, and all of this besides being a wine man and a fine man.

Practically all of the fascinating men I am writing about have had at least twenty-five years of experience in the wine field.

Brother Timothy, F.S.C., is Cellarmaster and Vice President at Christian Brothers. Brother Tim is the handsome man shown in living color or black and white ads on the pages of popular magazines, depicting the glories of Christian Brothers' wines, champagnes and brandy. He is the best salesman they have. He invariably photographs just the way an advertising man would hope — there is Brother surrounded by wine casks, a few bottles of wine and a half-filled glass nearby, giving the impression that he's much too busy making certain the wines are aging properly to do any more nipping than occupationally necessary.

I was delighted to find firsthand that Brother Timothy does drink a glass or two of wine when he is out of that cellar and the photographer's lights!

He is a loved man and it is every wine man's wish that he doesn't actively retire from his winery and publicity duties with the Brothers for many more years.

A winemaker with possibly no peer in the California red wine field is Louis M. Martini. He is a part of California wine history and received the American Society of Enologists' Merit

Award at their 1972 convention. (Some of his Napa Valley vintner colleagues, led by Beaulieu's Andre Tchelistcheff, had scheduled a private after-the-award-ceremonies party for him but had to cancel the affair almost at the last minute; they feared it would have been too much excitement, in one day, for the grand, eighty-five-year-old gentleman.)

Adolph Heck, the perennially suave looking President of F. Korbel & Bros. Winery, is the eldest son of a wine-making family. 'Dolph is a dynamo, knows what he wants and does it. He's kept Korbel champagnes high on the most desired list since he and his brothers, Paul and Ben, took over the company in the mid 1950s. Now he's going all out for promoting his still wines, instead of letting them merely coast along in the shadow of the champagnes.

If 'Dolph likes you, a sure indication is your being called "Musclehead."

Rodney Strong, Chairman of the Board of Windsor Vineyards, has helped bring the somewhat provincial County of Sonoma to its feet over his success at public relations. Rod's wine mail-order promotion skyrocketed and that, with personalized labels, has helped insure his winery's good fortune. He admits that he never thought the personalized wine label on the bottle would be such a phenomenal success because it had been tried before and got only limited attention. Rod's individualized salesmanship, his energy and drive, coupled with his personable wife, Charlotte, all help him become a winner.

Getting to be a trademark with Charlotte are her lightly tinted glasses and I've also heard about Rod's pet golden eagle, appropriately dubbed "Rommel."

Myron Nightingale, a king in all-around wine making, is now winemaster at Beringer. Ask almost any other winemaker about him and the description will be: "a hell of a winemaker." He and his red-haired wife, Alice, bring a lot of zip to the enology convention parties and it's easy to remember their last name. I enjoy hearing Myron paged: "Calling Mr. Nightingale."

Andre Tchelistcheff was winemaster for Beaulieu Vineyards even years and years before it was acquired by Heublein's. Andre, a dapper, continental type, is one of the most quoted experts in the California wine business. For several years he has been thinking of at least semiretirement, and in early 1973 he made the decisive move. Now Andre can devote time to other wineries as a consultant. His hand-picked successor, Dick Peterson, with a Ph.D. in agricultural chemistry, is no newcomer to the wine field. He's already had fifteen years of experience in top management.

Andre's son, Dimitri, is a winemaker for the highly-thought-of Bodegas de Santo Tomas in Ensenado, Mexico.

Ed Norman has been, for the past twenty-four years, super salesman of corks, bottles, labels, bottling, filling, and corking machinery to wineries, plus being confidant and cheerer-upper to winery management personnel by the hundreds. Ed, with his booming voice and optimistic outlook, is one salesman whose visits are eagerly awaited.

There is probably no other person in California's wine business who is the custodian of so many secrets about other wine people, about wineries, about the real reason a person left a winery or was asked to leave, about mergers that will take place, about anything that someone wants to tell another and yet be certain his revelation will go no further. Like a perfectly fitted cork in a bottle, Ed is a part of the wine scene that just wouldn't be the same without him.

Although no Californian, but a native of Hammondsport, New York, Walter Taylor should be included in the listing of fabulous men in the wine business. Now owner of Bully Hill Vineyards, he is the grandson of the founder of Taylor Wines. Walter is a maverick and was, not politely at all, booted out of Taylor's Great Western Division as Executive Vice President, when he dared open his mouth to the press about how he believed New York State wines could do a great deal to better their product.

He is the leader of the small group (but he's vocal enough for all) which is attempting to get laws passed enforcing wines designated as from New York State being made from grapes grown only in that state. As it stands now, as much as twenty-five percent of the wine may come from California and still be permitted to be labeled as a New York State wine. Also, a certain amount of water and sugar may be added in making the wines; this also need not be put on the label.

Walter is for truth in labeling and purity in wine making. And he's trying to prove it will all pay off, as witness his vintage estate-bottled wines of Bully Hill.

After the repeal of Prohibition there was a tremendous task

facing the wine industry. New vineyards had to be planted, old ones replanted, wine stocks built up and the biggest problem of all: educate the public about the merits of wine and get them to switch from strong spirits.

In California, the one organization that led in promotion of wines and wine consumption is called the Wine Institute.

The industry believed that if Americans could be informed of the nature and uses of wines, millions of people would recognize and use this oldest of natural mealtime beverages.

So in 1938 the wine growers, with the cooperation of the California Department of Agriculture, approved the first of the wine marketing orders which have been renewed continually.

The Marketing Order for Wine is one hundred percent financed by per-gallon assessments on California wines prepared for market. Funds are administered by the Wine Advisory Board, made up of representative growers.

The Wine Advisory Board conducts national educational, promotional, medical research, advertising and general merchandising programs for the wines of California. National publicity and research are carried out by the Wine Institute under contract to the Wine Advisory Board.

Everyone connected with the Wine Institute and the Wine Advisory Board goes all-out to help each winery, no matter the size. President of the Wine Institute now is Harry Serlis, with many previous years of wine experience. Don McColly, president of the Institute from 1937 until he resigned in 1969, is still very active in the wine field.

When there are so many talented (and personable) people in both the Institute and Advisory Board as Roy Taylor, Jack Matthews, and Larry Cahn, anyone connected with a winery is bound to feel that these people are gung ho to promote California wines.

Another group, privately funded, and founded in 1949, is the American Society of Enologists. Its primary function is "to communicate scientific information among those concerned with research and development in enology and viticulture." The ASE is considered so elite that enologists and viticulturists come from all over the world to attend the yearly three-day convention. A few of the guiding lights of the ASE are Min Akiyoshi, Jim Guymon, Hector Castro, and George Cooke.

The men and women of the Wine Institute, Advisory Board,

and ASE go a long way toward helping the personnel of the individual wineries become cognizant that someone really cares.

I have been able to list only a limited number of the fabulous people in the wine industry; however, I salute them all with, *"A votre santé!"*

CHAPTER XII

WHAT DO WINE PEOPLE DRINK?

I used to believe that anyone who worked for a winery knew all about wine. My first realization that this was erroneous thinking came when an eight-year veteran winery worker asked me for a tour because he'd never known what was really in the rooms other than the two where he worked. He also requested a wine tasting because he had had the company's product only at the annual Christmas party; otherwise he drank whiskey.

Soon I accepted the fact that the billing clerk might know the spelling of the varietal wines but that didn't mean she'd ever tasted them. I even got used to my disappointment over some executives who never drank wine unless around people they felt they had to impress.

For some winery management personnel, drinking while at work is part of the job. My position at Almadén practically required going around with glass in hand, whether ever refilled nobody could be certain. In fact, it became such a part of the scenery to watch me escorting visitors about the winery while balancing glass by stem that, when I arrived sans glass, the gossip was: "Well! She's not working today!"

The format was, immediately after greeting our VIPs, to pour champagne or sherry and, glass in hand, start the tour. Sometimes the butler would meet us midway with a cart containing fresh glasses and more iced champagne. Because of this, the tours occasionally became quite lively.

Louie Benoist was the best salesman of his product. In all my years at Almadén I never met anyone who could consume so much wine and other spirits and yet remain the same personality.

At the end of a thirteen-hour day of entertaining, I'd be sipping Perrier water with Mrs. Benoist while Mr. B would be having one last Brandy Extraordinaire. He would be talking about ideas for such and such a winery project and making suggestions as to how I could help formulate them. I would let his words go in one ear and out the other, figuring these were merely thoughts of a tired man.

Yet Louie remembered everything he said and right down to the last detail. He was also always the first one up in the morning and he never seemed to need sunglasses.

Benoist drank a lot of champagne, and often, before lunch, he had cocktail sherry. Generally, though, it was champagne before the meal, after the meal, and between meals. Every once in awhile he would get on a martini kick but even a number of these seemed not to bother him.

I've been told that wineman John Felice always gets an awed audience recalling the afternoon he went to Almadén to pick black olives for marinating and, just as he was about to depart with his haul, he was sighted by Benoist and invited for a drink. From what I understand, John says it was the biggest mistake he ever made. How he got home that night he still doesn't know, but he clearly remembers that, aside from little patches of red on his cheeks, Benoist showed no sign of the amount he'd imbibed. From what I hear, John also states that he fed two martinis each to at least three of the potted plants on the terrace.

"Vinegar" Dan Bagnani (who recently sold his Geyser Peak Winery to Schlitz Brewing Company) has mentioned he had the same experience several times with Benoist, each time vowing it would be the last. But Louie Benoist is such great company and the surroundings of Almadén so relaxing that it was a difficulty of the first magnitude to refuse the invitation to "have a little refresher."

It didn't take long before I began to recognize signals as to what kind of a drinking day to expect. When the butler began taking ice cubes by tongs and tinkling them into the glasses of champagne held by the Benoists, I immediately knew the party, and my day, could be more than ten hours. Contrary to what one would expect, the ice cubes do not distort the taste or the bubbles of the champagne. Actually, they intensify both the taste and the sparkle — unless you wait until the cubes are melted before drinking.

Though they had all types of alcoholic spirits available, the Benoists were wine drinkers and connoisseurs.

Most wine men are oriented toward all kinds of liquor. They have a high tolerance for alcohol and great control. However, possibly because they are around wines most of the time, when partying they prefer something other than wine.

The overall favorite is brandy: on the rocks or with soda. Two very prominent winemakers, who are likewise long-time buddies, sometimes get together on vacation and will start the day off, and wind it up, by drinking cocktail sherry, chase it with brandy, then more sherry followed by brandy, etc. The fish being angled don't seem to mind, their wives don't object, and the men's cast-iron stomachs haven't rebelled yet. It's only the people who drop by for a visit who don't understand how they can do it.

I've noticed, on the mornings-after at wine conventions, that Bloody Marys are popular. And, at an open-house breakfast party in his suite, Alan Hemphill of Korbel introduced me to a certain eyeopener and quick picker-upper: grapefruit juice and champagne. Recipe: take nine or ten ounce glass, half fill with grapefruit or orange juice, finish filling with iced champagne. Ummmmm!

An even better hangover rule to follow is trying to prevent it. The trick is to know that you've drunk too much and then, before going to bed, take two aspirins with just enough water to down them and then two tablespoonsful of pure bee's honey. It always works. The awful "what have I done to myself" mental and physical tortures are greatly lessened.

The California Wine Institute holds three big meetings yearly. There is the spring meeting, the June luncheon and champagne reception-dinner dance, and the December Palm Springs convention.

Besides the luncheons, dinners and champagne parties listed on the itinerary, several firms doing business with the wineries always are on hand to welcome everyone in special rooms set up for partying. Wine, unless it be champagne, is never offered. The usual vodka, Scotch, whiskey, gin and brandy are on the serving table. Brandy highballs are the favorites with gin and tonic or vodka and tonic taking second position. I've tried figuring it out; maybe brandy is so popular because it has a wine base.

I learned — or rather didn't learn — the hard way how brandy is made. The articles I'd read simply did not get through to me and, after having asked two winemakers to explain the brandy process and still not understanding, I decided, temporarily, to forego that bit of knowledge.

Then, at a Wine Institute dinner dance I sat at the same table as Adolph Heck of Korbel. They make brandy and I figured surely this man could state the operation in simple language. 'Dolph was very considerate and patient; he went over every point, in elementary language, of what had heretofore been a mystery. He had me repeat what I'd learned and was pleased with his pupil. I had to tell my escort, as we two-stepped on the dance floor, all about making brandy.

The next morning, while brushing my teeth, I started mentally going over my new information and quickly discovered that I had a memory block; the facts I had so proudly gathered had either vaporized or become so watered down as to be useless — all on account of my having drunk brandy!

The late wine broker Bob Salles's suite of rooms was always a meeting place for wine people and their friends to unwind and learn the latest bit of news about one another. A number of business deals were also made at these after-the-meeting-is-over parties.

Perennially hosting some hospitality room at all the conventions is genial Ed Norman, Executive Vice President of FP Packaging. Wine men and their friends are assured that wherever Ed is, there is good liquor, good talk, and pleasant and relaxing surroundings.

The biggest get-together of wine people is held the end of June at the annual convention of the American Society of Enologists. When the ASE started convening, in 1949, there were few members and it was truly a wine industry family get-together. Now it has grown to about seven hundred members with almost ninety percent of these managing to get to the convention for at least one day out of the three. However, many members still bring their families and combine business with a week's vacation. It is especially welcome when the convention is held at places such as Del Coronado Hotel near San Diego or in Santa Barbara. This means that the great number of ASE members who live around the San Francisco Bay area can get to a resort hotel and enjoy a change of scenery.

There is always some extra partying going on at this convention. If you don't attend the daily symposiums, you can expect to find a hospitality room open or merely visit with a friend or new acquaintance at the bar or poolside, or maybe share a bottle of champagne with a member who has brought along a case.

Officially the convention starts on a Thursday at 1:00 P.M. and ends with an Awards Banquet on Saturday night. Unofficially the convention gets under way several days before and hardly anyone leaves before Sunday afternoon.

Each night there is some especially big party. On Thursday, the welcoming rooms of companies catering to the wine industry are going strong.

Friday night is the BIG BASH, given for the past ten years by the Cincinnati-based chemical manufacturing company of Fries & Fries. It starts about 10:00 P.M. and an hour later it is extending down the hallways. Trying to get another drink, or even the first, proves that you have lots of perseverance.

Sales Director John Hernstat and his wife, Nancy, should get medals for the years of bartending, bulldozing paths to restrooms for those in need, and for courage enough to come back to serve the thirsty groups of winemakers year after year after year. Technical Coordinator Cy Seilkop is a bachelor. Since he too plays host at that and similar company open-house parties year around, it is understandable; he is tired.

On Saturday, after the champagne reception overflowing with viticulture and enology students, besides the full-time convention attendees, there is the Awards Banquet and, after that, another Fries & Fries party. But, on this night, to many the Fries affair is superseded by Johnny Franzia's champagne party. It has become an enology convention tradition.

Sunday morning there is intense quiet in the sections of the hotel where the conventioneers are housed and I perceptibly learned not to go pounding on someone's door, calling, "Are you ready to take me to Mass?" One phones and doesn't let the phone ring too long.

By 10:30 A.M. there are a few silent and somber wine men in the dining room hoping they may order Bloody Marys or brandy floats with Cointreau. The only early risers are those with a plane to catch. The line-up at the check-out desk begins around noon. Some lucky souls can stay in bed that long and then leave the next day after spending a more moderate evening out.

Other than at business meetings, not many parties are given by wine men for wine men. Oh, there are some men who have been friends for years and they and their families will vacation together, but there are few parties composed primarily of wine people.

Al and Ruth Pucchinelli usually give two a year. Al, supposedly retired, once owned vineyards in Santa Clara County and has remained active in the wine industry. The Pucchinellis now live in Sonoma County. Their parties are comprised of eight to ten couples in the wine business. It's a select group that attends these gatherings. The talk is wine, wine people and family.

When the Mirassous throw a party, it's done at the winery and is a festive occasion. Norbert and Ed, Steve and Dan, and the assorted Mirassou family and in-laws know how to put on a show.

One that will linger in many a mind was the Mexican Fiesta held in the tasting room. Dinner was served in the bottling room, and through it all a Mariachi band kept everyone beating the tempo with their champagne glasses clinking.

One still-discussed, after-a-convention meeting party held in a suite of rooms had a quizzical and then humorous ending. It was way in the wee hours. A dozen winemakers were still chatting and sipping and two or three wives had decided to stick it out. Suddenly, three fresh female faces emerged and the newly arrived girls sidled up to the men, asking their names. The winemen, according to Myron Nightingale, were mentally questioning if the girls were wives they hadn't met.

The newcomers had a drink and then a few minutes later Mrs. Mike (Ruth) Bo loudly reminded, "Listen, everybody. Remember, you're all invited to my place for breakfast and champagne." (This was an annual breakfast at the Bo's.)

One of the girls piped up, "Where do you live?"

Ruth, "In Gilroy."

Girl, "What the hell are you doing working this territory?"

The mystery of the girls was no longer mysterious!

After seven years of going to conventions and being invited to a number of private parties, I pretty well knew what wine people preferred and what they would drink.

Consequently, I looked with interest at the drinking habits of the new executives taking over Almadén, the top men of National Distillers.

It was love at first sight, before I even knew his wine preference, upon seeing Bev Ohlandt, Vice Chairman of the Board of Directors of National Distillers and then Chairman of the Board of Directors of Almadén. He looked just like I had always pictured a super whiskey salesman: beautifully groomed, an expensive cigar in hand, ruddy cheeks and a fantastic personality. Even though Bev did not walk around with an Old Grand Dad on the rocks in hand, he did carry in his breast pocket the Dunhill cigars I expected.

Also, much to my delight, it took him only a couple of months and he began to acquire at least a semifondness for sherry.

John E. Bierwirth, the Chairman of the Board of National Distillers, is another story. Dear one he may be, but it's always orange juice. Straight. Maybe over the rocks, but no alcohol added.

After much checking and musing, I came to the conclusion that Mr. Bierwirth probably wanted to make triply certain that he wouldn't mix up on any meetings of the seventeen or so boards of directors of which he is a member. I've yet to find out if one of them has anything to do with Minutemaid or Sunsweet.

CHAPTER XIII

PERSONAL PREFERENCES

I have two favorite drinks: Pernod and champagne.

Pernod became my apéritif choice when I lived in New Orleans. I was introduced to it at the Old Absinthe House which specialized in Absinthe drips. Even though it was by then contraband in the United States, I sometimes had the real Absinthe — the drink of such famed men as Toulouse-Lautrec, Lafcadio Hearn, and O'Henry, and a favorite of New Orleanians, whether poets, artists, writers, or soldiers of fortune.

For those who drank too heavily, the wormwood narcotic in Absinthe had a habit of eventually driving them insane. Consequently, the drink became outlawed in Europe and finally, around World War I, in New Orleans. Then, although the wormwood was removed from the recipe and the name changed to either Pernod or Herbsaint, the liqueur retained its licorice and anise flavor and hence the allure for me. (Given a choice between a superb French pastry and a bag of black licorice buttons, I will opt for the buttons.)

After three Pernods I've had it. Its distinctive taste wanes and I keep reminding myself I should have stopped at two.

Champagne is something else. I can continue to drink it without my taste buds becoming tired or jaded. I can sip it anytime, as long as it is very cold and preferably a Brut or Blanc de Blancs.

It was during Louie Benoist's reign that Almadén champagne became known worldwide. Through Benoist's social and business connections and Pete Jurgens's salesmanship with wholesalers and retailers, Almadén was used at Presidential Inaugural Balls and at the White House, Blair House, at governors' mansions, at U.S. Embassies abroad, at debutante balls, and at get-togethers of the nation's leading chefs. In blind tastings of wine connoisseurs it was picked as the top-rated champagne so often that sometimes I waxed less voluble in telling about the honor after honor that came Almadén's way.

The bottle even had its own distinguished tissue wrapper. Designed by the French artist Oscar Fabrés, it depicted in gold on a white background an ice bucket holding a magnum of champagne with cork popping. Carrying the bucket and bubbly in midair flight are two angels, naked but for grape leaf wreaths around their heads and some strategically placed clusters of leaves below the waist. Bobbing around the bucket are several floating champagne glasses ready to be filled.

The glasses were always filled at Almadén. Even the bubbles were in greater profusion. The bottle-fermenting method used in making the champagne automatically insured not only smaller bubbles but more of them; and lots of the glasses were scratched.

Unbelievable as it may seem, putting a scratch in the form of an X or a Z (remember the mark of Zorro?) in the bottom of the bowl of the glass provides an incentive for the champagne to become more bubble prone. I discovered this over on the Benoists' terrace while hosting a group of foreign dignitaries. Somehow or other I managed to find a second or two to muse, simultaneously glancing downward into my glass of champagne. It was almost emptied and I noted the expensive crystal had a perceivable scratch in the bottom. I got a fresh glass and took only a few sips before I again saw a similar mark. I chalked it up to careless in-for-the-day extra help.

A week or so later, while over at the Benoists' and chatting with the butler who was drying glasses, I mentioned the scratched ones. He then explained that if there is a roughness in the glass, the bubbles will continue forming long after the champagne ordinarily would be on the flat side. And, when the champagne bottle is newly opened, the bubbles will be in greater abundance than usual if in contact with a scratch. As in the hollow-stem champagne glasses, where the bubbles are more noticeable, so also with an irregular surface.

Since the bubbles are the main difference between champagne and a still wine, I hurried out and bought a diamond cutter and started designing Xs and Zs.

I can't remember when I didn't love champagne. When I first started dating, unaware I could specify a glass of champagne sans a sugar cube, I had champagne cocktails. Invariably the first time my escort heard the words "champagne, please" in answer to his: "What will you have, Mary?" he would go into minor shock at the thought of his wallet. There was always a surprised relief at discovering this drink really wasn't any more expensive than a good Scotch or bourbon and water.

In fact, I consistently noted, with rare exceptions, that an escort minded not at all if you had four or five drinks at $1.50 per; but if you mentioned champagne, he would blanch, even though a split (two glasses) went for $1.50 and you drank only four glasses all evening.

Aware of the fact I could freely obtain as much as needed, I decided, when going to work for Almadén, to fun experiment with the bubbly. I washed in champagne. I rinsed my hair in champagne. I brushed my teeth in champagne.

Only once.

It took merely that one try to emphatically convince me champagne is for drinking. Anna Held may have bathed in champagne but she was a very sticky girl afterwards. And toothpaste and champagne simply don't mix!

Learning about champagne was fascinating and fun for me and I lost no time in acquiring the essential knowledge and every other tidbit of information.

It is of paramount importance that champagne be served very cold, about thirty-nine to forty degrees. At first my champagne was not properly chilled. It always tasted so much better at the Benoists that I logically figured a special vintage had been kept for the boss's use. After one elegant party on the terrace, I inquired of Al Huntsinger if I could get some of Benoist's private stock. To my surprise, Al informed me there was no special champagne reserve; what went to the Main House, my cottage, the butler's pantry, the retailer, all came from the same wine and aging cellars. After a few questions, Al deducted that my icebox wasn't cold enough. He was correct; my box was at forty-eight degrees, fine for the white wines but by no means cold enough for champagne. He set it to thirty-five degrees, and from then on the champagne I poured was delightful.

I was lucky; I had two iceboxes: one for wines and one for food. If you set the temperature dial to thirty-five degrees in the family icebox, the "happening" will be my experience — you'll end up with frozen raw eggs.

The trick is either to have a small extra icebox that you can regulate to a constant thirty-four to thirty-five degrees, since the champagne comes out a few degrees higher, or keep the champagne in the regular icebox for at least three hours, and then thirty minutes before serving put it in the freezer compartment.

Champagne can also be rapidly chilled to the proper degree by putting it from room temperature (sixty-eight degrees) directly into the freezer and keeping it there for an hour and a half or so. The one danger in this latter method is to forget the time and — voila! — you could be faced with (a) one frozen block in the shape of a champagne bottle or, worse yet, (b) an explosion. I have suffered both.

The most enjoyable bottle of champagne I've ever had was one that had been left for a few hours in a snowbank at Yosemite. When dug out to be enjoyed with *pâté* and chicken sandwiches, it beat all I had served, even in Baccarat.

Ollie Goulet, Almadén's former winemaster, dreamed up a novel, clever, yet practical showmanship manner of offering champagne. Occasionally he'd give a party for thirty or more. Instead of having champagne stored for chilling all over the neighborhood or ice buckets by the dozens about, Ollie ordered a truckload of shaved ice, had it dumped on the lawn or patio, and stuck in dozens of bottles of champagne neck down so that the cold bottles, when needed, could be pulled and corks popped by the guests.

Everybody who visited Almadén liked champagne, even if they hadn't previously been a fan of that beverage. Not to be excluded were the gophers who drank it with relish.

There were two long-lived, persistent little brown-furred members of the gopher clan that had staked claim to my backyard and who won out over the gardener's efforts to eradicate them. They became so friendly and fearless that they often openly sat in at my weekend barbeques. This both amused and startled the guests, and prompted one to proffer a drink of his champagne. Kneeling, tipping the glass sideways, he slowly reached toward the gopher. Sir Gopher practically walked into the glass, sipping all the while. He stopped when he'd had enough and scampered back into his hole.

From that time on, we had performing gophers, appearing almost every party. Toward the end of the summer one must have taken too much for his gopher-system we thought, because after having drunk a total of about two ounces during an afternoon, he took off never to reappear. The other, or a close-resembling relative, was still in my backyard when I left.

*   *   *   *   *

To insure getting your money's worth, never keep a bottle of champagne, once you've pulled the cork, longer than twenty-four hours. It goes flat rapidly. You're paying dearly for those bubbles and the idea is to enjoy them. Once in a while a bottle that had been opened more than a day held up well enough to please most visitors — especially the ones who weren't used to champagne. But I made it a point, and likewise instructed my help, to use up the opened bottles first. Most tasting rooms will not hold over an opened bottle to the following day. Likewise, a few minutes before closing time they will not open a fresh bottle for tasting room use.

Champagne is heavily taxed. There is a federal tax of $3.40 per gallon, adding up to a little more than $8.00 per case plus the state tax. (The tax on a dry still wine is seventeen and one-half cents per gallon, twenty times less than on the bubbly.)

Why should champagne at twelve percent alcohol have such a vastly different tax rate than a still wine of the same alcohol content?

Nobody knows how it really came about, except the unusually steep tax had its start at the beginning of the twentieth century. In those days only the top-hatted, white-tie-and-tails set sipped this luxury drink, and the federal government considered the rich fair game for the tax levies. Probably the thinking went that if you could afford to drink champagne, you had to be wealthy and therefore deserved to pay dearly. Then, of course, once a tax gets tacked on, how often does it get lowered?

The best champagne buy I have ever encountered, combining quality and price, is Le Domaine, Almadén's less expensive brand. It is one of two or three noncostly champagnes produced in the U.S. that is fermented in the bottle.

There is a difference between the French method of fermentation and the Bulk process.

The French method means the original way of making champagne, discovered by the monk Dom Perignon, in the latter part of the seventeenth century. If a winery is going to spend the money for this lengthy, laborious process, the grapes used for the still wine will be some of the best.

In the original French method of fermentation, the *cuvée* (which is the still wine ingredient — either one kind of grape or a blend) is mixed with sugar and yeast to start a second fermentation. Empty, sterilized bottles are filled with this combination and then the bottles are stacked in a room kept at a temperature of about sixty degrees. It takes some eight weeks for the second fermentation to take place, while the bottled wine builds up to a pressure of one hundred twenty-five pounds per square inch.

At Almadén, the bottles were ingeniously stacked to prevent a chain reaction when one bottle did blow. The reason for their exploding was an impediment in the glass that couldn't withstand the pressure. (A note to remember: an unopened bottle of champagne should be handled with caution. Accidents can happen when the bottle is too warm or was shaken up on its way from icebox to table, and the cork may pop out prematurely and hurt an eye besides releasing a spray of champagne over everyone and everything. Always open the bottle with the neck pointed away from yourself or anyone else, just in case.)

After the wine has become champagne, it is left in bottles to age for several years, all the while building up bubbles, bubbles. The bubbles count a lot. The more bubbles and the smaller the bubbles usually denotes bottle fermenting, bottle aging for a long time. The longer the champagne is bottle aged, the smaller the bubbles and the longer they last in the glass.

Next time when ordering a glass of champagne at your favorite lounge, take a good look at the bubbles. It's surprising. Some as large around as sugar peas will pop and do a disappearing act as fast as a blink of the eye. Some will last only a few minutes and then the champagne will be flat.

When the bubbles don't endure long, unnoticed, though, by most people because they drink so fast, it is generally champagne made by the Bulk process. This method will say on the label: Charmat or Bulk. Making champagne this way means mixing still wine, sugar and yeast in a tank (rather than individual bottles) of about one thousand gallons and leaving it there to ferment for about a week to ten days. Presto, champagne! It is ready for bottling and immediate sale. Buying champagne labeled Charmat or Bulk is almost always less expensive. Usually it's corked with a plastic cork that costs about a cent and one-half instead of with a wood cork at six cents; its label and foil will not be as costly, and the bottle will be thinner and less strong.

Charmat process champagne can be very good but most champagne fans prefer the original French method.

In a newspaper interview, Count De Vogue, the managing director of France's famed Moët et Chandon champagne house, surprised the reporter by stating that the best market for champagne was England. The reason he gave was there is no sun in England and, since the people need to be warmed up, the British drink champagne to see life in a better light.

How true. Gloomy people do not drink champagne and stay gloomy.

Songs, plays and verse extol the gaiety of champagne.

Noel Coward in his play *Private Lives* popularized champagne as the drink of the sophisticates; the zany Spike Jones's recording of "Cocktails for Two" certainly wasn't about a Dubonnet-on-the-rocks. There is a decisive, unforgettable popping of a cork that can only mean champagne.

Collett's play *Gigi*, when made into a movie, brought forth the hummable song, "The Night They Discovered Champagne." And, in the Peter Sellers movie *Pink Panther*, one of the songs is called "Champagne and Quail," a good combination on anyone's menu.

There is Lawrence Welk's famous "Champagne Lady." Champagne beige is a favorite color of brides as well as other members of the wedding party, while a champagne blowout means a festive party to end all parties.

All these mentionings of champagne, in the final analysis, add up to the fact that champagne has rightfully come to be popularly known and accepted as the alcoholic beverage to choose for life's lightest, finest and most important moments.

Cheers!

CHAPTER XIV

THE TAKEOVER OF "MY" WINERY AND OTHERS

As in any relationship that is going along smoothly, a relaxed mind is seldom thinking about a dissolution of the business or a third party causing a disruption.

When it does happen, the name of the culprit is usually MONEY.

So it is in the wine industry. Lack of money can force a sale and the potential for making money can lure a buyer.

In California today there are about two hundred and twenty-five bonded wineries and seven of them collectively produce approximately seventy-five percent of the wine marketed. Some two dozen are medium-size wineries; the rest are classified as small (ranging from fifty to two hundred acres).

During Prohibition most of the wineries were forced to plow under, sell their land, or go bankrupt. However, about one hundred survived by making either sacramental wine for religious use or by selling to individuals for medicinal consumption. Since the government allowed the head of a household to make two hundred gallons of wine per year for his own use, the vineyards kept a trade going by selling fresh grapes to those home winemakers.

Immediately after the repeal of Prohibition, the wine

141

industry had a boom and by 1936 there were eight hundred bonded premises. It appeared everyone was trying to cash in on the resurgence of its popularity. Not all made a success in the wine business; there was great competition and many of the wines were not of a good enough quality to compete on the market. However, anyone who was able to hold out until World War II made money, either by selling the land or the wine on hand. Since obtaining stronger alcohol was next to impossible, wine sales had another bonanza — until 1947 when the bottom dropped out of the market.

It was a buyer's market; the wine had to be sold. In 1948 there were 443 wineries and by 1961 this had dwindled to 241.

The smaller premium wineries continued to prosper and found a ready market. It was the medium-size operations that could not compete; especially with superior marketing skills such as those of Gallo's.

Yet the past dozen years have found even more and more people wanting to get into the wine picture. The big companies take over medium-size wineries because they figure there is money to be made; the private individual buys a small winery or starts his own because of the love of wine making and the willingness to put in ninety-hour weeks on something of his own.

There are still a number of small "mom and pop" operations, but they are rapidly disappearing. Old age is coming upon the present owners and they don't care to continue working the long hours, or the children don't want to remain in the business, so they sell. Nonetheless, these small wineries of fifty to two hundred acres have a waiting list of other buyers who would like to start their own family grape-growing, wine-making heritage.

Unless one remains quite small and employs few personnel other than family, there is little money made that doesn't have to be plowed back into the business. Making fine wine is expensive. There is so much equipment that must be bought in order to insure quality wines that it is nothing to put a million dollars into a small winery. And before the loan is paid off, there is more to be bought: casks, fermenting tanks, improvements in the tasting room, wind machines to keep the frost from killing the vines. The list keeps growing; there must be a tremendous love of the business and a willingness to sacrifice personally.

The two dozen or so moderately sized wineries are mostly premium and independently owned. However, one of the best known, Beaulieu, was acquired a few years back by Heublein. Wisely, though, it is allowed to continue operating almost as when privately owned. Inglenook, also a Heublein subsidiary, seems to have actually improved in quality. This is conceded even by those wags who were first to remark after the acquisition, "Well, there goes another premium winery downhill."

Louie M. Martini refuses to sell. Some wine buffs are betting that when octogenarian Louie M. goes, his son, Louie P., could accept a top money offer — provided, of course, that he stays on, the winery name continues and the quality remains the best. There are likewise those who believe no Martini would ever allow an outsider to take over the beloved family business.

The Mirassou Winery is one medium-size premium that at least has little of a labor problem; they've got so many in the family (even their seven- and eight-year-old children take an interest) they can cut money corners.

Other medium-size independents include Sebastiani, Krug, Concannon, Parducci, Novitiate, and Korbel.

Would-be buyers keep hoping the owners of Korbel will eventually acquiesce to their offers. (Korbel is so highly esteemed that pressure is continually on the Heck family to sell.) Rumor has it that Korbel only recently came a signature away from being sold. It is reported the contract was on the desk of 'Dolph Heck, President of Korbel. He supposedly had pen in hand poised to write.

Suddenly, 'Dolph put the pen down, got out of his chair, and murmured, "No ... no, thanks. I just can't give up the family business."

United Vintners, since 1969 a subsidiary of Heublein, is the second largest producer of wine grapes in California. The largest wine producer in the U.S., Gallo, now produces over one hundred million gallons per year and United Vintners in 1972 marketed fifty million gallons. (The entire U.S. puts out about three hundred forty million gallons annually.)

In 1970, the Swiss food company, Nestle, bought Beringer Bros., a respected, almost century-old premium winery in Napa. It had become just too much for the remaining family to continue to operate while keeping up with the demand and the times.

Wente Brothers has no intention of selling. They are one of the few who have enough capital so they don't have to eat beans every other night in order to pay for another sprinkler. Not many independently owned wineries can make this claim. It is taking more and more money to operate successfully and turn a profit. Large companies can come up with the sizeable sums needed to insure a successful future, but few medium-size wineries have avenues of escape other than selling.

Christian Brothers is the only independent of the giant premiums. Both Almadén, the leader in premium sales, and Paul Masson have been bought out. Masson, taken over by Seagrams in 1955, had a changeover in their sales organization in early 1971, possibly because they were not keeping up with the phenomenal sales figures of Almadén. Hence, Brown Vintners was formed as the sales organization for Masson.

I became so accustomed to seeing pictures of Paul Masson and hearing about him while at Almadén that he truly became part of "the family." He died in the late 1930s and there are still many residents of the Santa Clara Valley who vividly remember him. I just didn't like a somber tintype head-and-shoulders of him, with a stare (no doubt nearsighted) and pince-nez forever looking at me from my tasting room wall. I removed it, face downwards, to the shelf beneath the stored stereo tapes.

Before leaving Almadén, I hung on the walls a few mementoes of the past years. I am sorry I did not take them with me. They had been forgotten to all but a lover of history such as I. I had become a part of Almadén and its background was therefore part of me.

It was a sad parting and sudden for some. Almadén was sold to get more money to keep it as the number one premium wine producer.

At first, we thought Jock Whitney would buy us. He wanted to and because I had once met him at Hialeah, I could visualize trips to the race tracks and thoroughbreds training among the grape vines.

National Distillers and Chemical Corporation won out. The word was "the machinery" had arrived. This turned out to be some charming gentlemen from National Distillers. Even though they weren't "my" wine people, I began to like them. They were so simpatico it took only about a year before they didn't seem like outsiders to most of us "old hands."

Almadén, albeit minus the glamour Louie and Kay Benoist generated, has continued to turn out — to most everyone's surprise — some of the best wine in the United States. This is mainly due to the winemaster, Al Huntsinger, and the foresight of the present top management — Bill Dieppe, long-time executive of Almadén and now president, and his key men, John McClelland and Markus Friedlin. The National Distillers management let the wine people continue to run the winery.

Even the parties at the wine conventions reflect the changeovers of recent times. About four years ago I began to detect a subtle difference in the conviviality, the general but personalized conversation. Finally I noted it wasn't imagination but reality. There were many new people attending the parties, new in the sense they were not wine people. They were businessmen representing recently acquired companies. Instead of wine to sell, they might as well be peddling hand towels, soap, magnesium, ink. That "feeling" about the product wasn't there; they were attending the convention because they were now in the wine business and wanted to get information for their superiors in some distant state. Sometimes they were there as a semispy, watching, listening to the conversation of the employee of the subsidiary company.

It's not the same camaraderie feeling at the parties. It never can be. Because it is a changing world, a more money-conscious world, even the wine business must march in tempo. For some, it has taken longer to get in step. A few will make their own tune. The important cadence is the quality of the wine. So far, it has remained a beautiful arrangement.

CHAPTER XV

FOND REMEMBRANCES

At the 1973 Wine Institute luncheon in San Francisco, I sat at a table across from Bill Dieppe, President of Almadén. I was happy he tossed a few bon mots at me because this afforded an opportunity to study him and to conclude that being at the top has even enhanced his manly good looks. I found it difficult, around so many of the "old, familiar faces," to keep my mind on the guest speaker's words; it was so easy to drift into a reverie of days on the vineyard.

Bill seldom came down and when he did it was usually as leader of a bus full of distributors or prize-winning wine salesmen from throughout the nation. There was often champagne served on the sixty-mile ride from San Francisco to Los Gatos and by the time the men reached the winery they were doubly impressed with the lavish display and quality of the food. Moments after the bus stopped, Bill would be the first out. I'd be standing by waiting to politely and hospitably greet each person disembarking. Showmanship would win out if Bill had his way; he'd effortlessly scoop me up while simultaneously introducing me to the male visitors. I feared to squirm lest I fall the long distance to the ground. All the top sales executives with Almadén have been and are Bunyanesque size, and Dieppe is no exception. The only physically short executive was the boss — Louie Benoist.

Although I never took out a measuring stick, I figured him to be about five-foot-six. Benoist had a tailor so good that Louie's valet, Jimmy Hopkins (he had been Mr. Benoist's father's man in Virginia for years) would occasionally "borrow" the boss's clothes. They had a way of staying with Jimmy. Chuckling over the episode, Benoist once related how Jimmy was serving drinks aboard their plane and Benoist thought the suit he had on looked familiar, so he mentioned that he had one quite similar.

"No, Junior," (Jimmy could freely get away with such an intimate term as he considered Benoist, Sr., the elder) "this suit's not similar. It's the same. It's yours." With a man of such courage, Benoist had only respect.

Another time, around 9:00 P.M., Benoist received a phone call from "Trader Vic" Bergeron saying there was a Negro trying to get into Trader Vic's and insisting Mr. Louis Auguste Benoist had told him to go there and charge everything. Furthermore, reported the Trader, the man flashed open his suit coat and inside was the name: Louis A. Benoist.

Jimmy got into Trader Vic's in San Francisco that evening!

He was one of several characters at Almadén I had the pleasure of working with. I understand he hasn't changed his personality even though he's had several wives and various fortunes. Jimmy still, in money or marriages, does not discriminate because of race, religion, or creed.

I miss getting mail addressed to "Miss Alma Den." I miss going outside and seeing Benoist's personal flag flapping on the mast, indicating he was arriving and would be in residence for at least overnight. I miss being able, while taking special guests through the Main House, to peek into Benoist's closets and count the assortment of shoes all the same style: pumps with bows, from leathers to suedes to velvet to buckskin to patent. He even wore them on the yacht. But then he didn't have to climb around the sails so there was no need for regulation yachting shoes.

I have fond memories of sitting around my fireplace with Father Tom Terry, S.J., and several of his priest-teacher colleagues, arguing the merits of this and that wine and doing comparative tastings. Father Terry has a Ph.D. in Enology-Viticulture from the University of California at Davis but he seldom gets a chance to test his palate. He never even got the opportunity to make use of his degree because the Jesuits decided they needed his other talents even more and made him President of the University of Santa Clara.

There was the excitement of sometimes watching Almadén District Manager Rudy Windmiller perform a strong-man feat for the guests he'd brought down. Rudy could tear a metropolitan telephone book in two with his hands. He could also lift the solid oak table in my tasting room single-handed. There was often something special going on in my cottage to make the guests remember the visit to the vineyard vividly.

The St. John Indian dancers from the Gila River Reservation in Arizona visited the vineyards and they volunteered to perform gratis for the barbeque guests. Their visit, after the collection, was profitable. The boys all attend the Franciscan-run elementary-high school on the reservation and are outstanding performers of authentic Indian dances. All summer long the troupe, under the guidance of Brother Bernardine Brophy, O.F.M., tours the U.S. and foreign lands. In 1972 they toured the Orient.

Friends of Brother Brophy suggested the group stop by to see me with the hope I could allow them to put on a show during my parties. With no reluctance, I gave the affirmative signal and waited for my first meeting with Brother and the American Indians. The boys, jammed into two cars, looked almost like any other teen- or subteenagers. I repeat, "almost," because their faces had more character than boys even much older. They were also noticeably reserved.

That changed immediately upon getting out of jeans and shirts and into buckskins and *au naturel.* Their individual personalities came through and the veneer of reserve they affected around strangers was replaced by a camaraderie of brother Indians.

I didn't know what to expect on the initial visit and could only "play it by ear." Before ending my winery tour I had announced to the luncheon guests that there would be a surprise in store for them during the champagne hour preceding the meal: genuine Indian dancers.

When we were in my backyard and champagne had been poured, brown-robed Brother Brophy started talking about the mission school and the boys from the various tribes. Then the boys came onto center stage. Their scheduled four dances were never enough for the audience who instinctively realized they were witnessing numbers they would probably never have the opportunity to see again.

After their dances, Brother passed a basket. I tried doing my share by walking around with a giant-size salad bowl; I usually came out with more money than Brother. Some of the guests seemed a bit worried that, since I was custodian of the champagne and wines, they had best give a little cash for their entertainment!

Several women visitors, I discovered, had fascinating and rewarding professional occupations. The one who I think has the most enviable job of any woman in the wine field, Kathleen Bourke, is editor of *WINE Magazine*, London. Although through the years we have kept in touch via air mail, our only face-to-face meeting lasted less than an hour. Kathleen, on a tour of California wineries, was due to spend two or three hours at Almadén, but the woman guide taking her from Paul Masson's, some fifteen miles away, became confused in directions and showed up quite late after a two-hour drive over hills and through valleys. With Kathleen's tight schedule, this meant a hurry-up tour, a hurry-up bit of refreshment and a talk-fast conversation.

Even though it was a condensed visit, her personality was so outstanding that Kathleen's stopover is memorable. When perusing *WINE Magazine*, bear in mind the woman shown talking to the wine experts of the world, dining with the wine connoisseurs, tasting with the wine masters, is lovely to look at. It's tough to tell; K.C. Bourke likes others to be seen and makes a habit of being photographed with her back to the camera.

While watching the latest Pillsbury bake-off, I heard a name with a familiar ring announced as one of the judges. It was the Home Economist for Jewel Food Stores, Jane Armstrong. Pretty Jane doesn't just plan menus to whet the appetite of the buying public; she also gives guided tours of Europe and South America, lectures and is a good listener to boot. When she does speak, this girl knows the score.

When genial Jim Kaufman, Almadén's perennial PR director, phoned to say he was bringing by the famed cookbook writer, Nika Hazelton, I spent several hours looking up articles she'd written and tacking them about the tasting room as a welcome. Along with thousands of other fans, I think Nika can out-cook, out-recipe, out-write, and out-talk Julia Child. Nika is the artist's artist. Her husband Harold agrees. Beside the picture Jim took of us together, I have a recent magazine cutout showing Nika in a receiving line, wearing a black evening dress ornamented by waist length strands of pearls. With her hair braided in coils around her head, she looked every bit the German Baroness.

Marge Plamp barged in as a noontime walk-in. She and her friend drove away hours later after I learned Marge is considered by many to be one of the best whiskey tasters in all of the U.S. With Brown-Forman Distillers Corp., Marge has been written up by authors who hold her talents in awe; she is likewise so likeable that even the men who aren't tops in the field think she is great. The novelty for me was finding out she loves wine and was eager to learn all she could on this vacation-information trip. My queries about whiskey tasting were answered in detailed language understandable to any woman. Since greeting Marge, I decided not to give up on converting whiskey drinkers to at least considering the added value of wine.

We seldom served water at our parties. The exceptions were when someone felt faint (then, why not brandy?), if they couldn't get down their vitamin or medications minus water, or if they insisted. For the most part, if champagne were proferred, the thought of asking for water almost necessitated a cold shoulder.

Benoist had the perfect liberal European attitude about drinking, as he once said, "If you are big enough to hold a glass, no matter what your age, you're welcome."

It always worked beautifully. Those children who wanted to taste and weren't able to successfully tolerate the few ounces, promptly decided they needed a nap and the adults had temporary freedom of conviviality among their peers.

Louie delighted in retelling, with Kay adding asides, the story of how he sent his younger sister, a Superior of the exclusive Catholic Order of the Madames of the Sacred Heart, several cases of wine and champagne. He did this periodically. That particular delivery time the nun acting as portress was on an errand and Mother Superior Benoist answered the insistent ring at the convent's back door.

The fullback-type truck driver explained he had some wine for that address. Mother Benoist told him to please bring it in and leave it with her. His reply, "I don't move anything until I see the head madame."

Another personality woman was Muriel Neeman. I had met Muriel and her husband, Bob, through mutual friends before I entertained her as a VIP at Almadén. Muriel's first marriage had been to Horace Dodge (his second). She bore him a boy and a girl, but after twelve years of marriage she decided "enough!" Muriel took no alimony from Dodge and very few possessions. To the week he died, he remained constantly in weekly telephone contact with her.

Muriel and Bob live in Cuernavaca, Mexico, and probably entertain the cream of international society as much there as they did in Saratoga, California, during the 1950s and 1960s.

I especially remember Muriel telling me about the man she married after Dodge. One of the firms he had owned was Yardley's of London. That bit of information brought up the subject of perfumes. I told the background of the scent I was wearing, Mary Chess's Tube Rose, and how Anita Colby one day had whirled into the New Orleans *Item*, covering the city room with the fragrance and converting the hardened reporters into being her slaves. I decided that was the perfume for me and it became my favorite.

Muriel, while sipping her glass of champagne, casually noted that her husband had purchased for her as a birthday gift the firm of Mary Chess.

I became more alert to Muriel.

Always aware of the gastronomic fantasies of friends, going to an opening game of the Giants with her was a sought-after invitation. She invariably prepared, as if going to Ascot, the finest.

The Michel Weills are intimates of Muriel and Bob. In his San Francisco *Chronicle* column, Herb Caen wrote:

> Sentiment is not dead department. One chair at the big luncheon table in the French Club on Mason is always kept vacant till about 1:15 P.M. — in case Monsieur Michel Weill decides to show up.

However, try as she could, Muriel could never get Michel (whose forebears founded the fabled White House in San Francisco) to try an inexpensive bottle of California champagne. Then, the sneak test.

A jubilant Muriel phoned. The previous evening she had hosted, for eight, a bridge party and the usual gourmet supper. Joe Ridder, publisher of the San Jose *Mercury-News* was a guest. With the crepes she served, the bottle's label wrapped in a napkin, a sec champagne. Monsieur Weill pronounced it one of the finest he'd had in many a year.

Muriel beamed. She had reason to. It was one of California's least expensive: Almadén's Le Domaine Extra Dry. Another example of how even a French connoisseur can be conquered!

I recall the big to-do when Almadén first came out with the polyethylene champagne cork. Trader Vic's was one of the initial en masse buyers. As fate had it, they expected to use about fifty cases for a catered banquet. Naturally, this amount of wine bottles cannot be left unopened until the last hour. So, about five hours before needed, the staff started pulling off foil and wire clamps, leaving the corks intact for last minute popping. Alas, the combination of heat and the plastic started a combustion reaction culminating in almost all of the corks blown before the appointed serving time. There were a few captains who also blew their tops but, luckily, the Trader understood the risk inherent in any new innovation.

Because I was given advance notice of most arrivals of VIPs, I seldom played a guessing game about their occupation. However, one couple, complete with a Greek interpreter, was a mystery until almost our farewells. The wife spoke a few words of English; the husband, none. I was under the impression they owned a restaurant in Washington, D.C. Merely minutes before they were about to bid *adeau*, I asked, through the interpreter, the name of their restaurant or nightclub so I could send visitors there.

Even with the profusion of champagne, there were a few moments of silence. Finally, it became clear to all three that I was not jesting. I was sincere. I thought I was entertaining restaurateurs. The interpreter explained and everyone laughed a hearty, natural laugh; I was hostessing the Finance Minister of Greece and his wife!

Nostalgically I remember having peacock breast sandwiches and Blanc de Blancs with Songwriter Mort Greene and Mort vowing to immortalize the occasion in verse.

It was a pleasure giving up a Thanksgiving Day to show around Dr. Virginia Miles, the Vice President-Special Planning for Young & Rubicam, Inc. Virginia and her husband, Fred, Managing Editor of *Railway Age*, had only one day in which to tour their favorite winery and I couldn't say no. It paid off for me. I'd love to hop into Virginia's brain. This woman could really remake the world.

Jeanne Viner, some say Washington, D.C.'s most glamorous bachelor girl hostess, visited. It was mutual admiration at sight.

Jeanne is one of the greatest promoters of California wines: she serves them at practically all of her star-studded soirées. And, if she ever again marries, I hope she leaves my address with some of her suitor rejects.

I'll never forget having dinner in the Captain's Cabin of the cruiser U.S.S. *Topeka* with Captain and Mrs. William Montgomery. Dinner on board a ship is worth hoarding in the memory bank.

And I still retain some xeroxed copies of the thank-you notes sent to the then California Assemblyman George Milias (later the California Commissioner of Labor and presently a deputy administrator of the Federal Environmental Protection Agency) from other members of the Legislature after he gave each of them, at the end of the legislative year, a bottle of Almadén champagne (donated by guess who?) as a memento from his county.

To my delight, many newspaper people expressed a personal interest in wine by going out of their way to stop at the winery. Some of them were: Bill Rice of the Washington *Post*, Barbara Hansen, formerly of the Los Angeles *Herald Examiner* and now of the Los Angeles *Times*, and Abe Chanin of the Arizona *Daily Star*.

I miss being able to use the winery as a grand excuse for inviting old friends like Derick Daniels, Executive Editor of the Detroit *Free Press*; Stan Opotowsky, Managing Editor of the New York *Post*; George Beebe, Assistant Publisher of the Miami *Herald*; Al Neuharth, President, Gannett Newspapers; and Jeanne Voltz, *Woman's Day* Magazine Food Editor.

And, I wonder if I'll ever get another perfect opportunity to prove to the likes of Paul Conroy, Executive Editor of the San Jose *Mercury* and *News* that champagne is as refreshing as a martini. Paul brought along award-winning Ridder Publications Washington correspondent Al Eisele, who's the wine buff.

I miss hearing so many stranger-than-fiction true stories about famous people. Such as the one concerning the richer-than-rich socialite, one of the *grande dames* of America, who, while at her Nassau estate, summoned from all corners of the U.S. a barrage of lawyers to work out some complicated legal matters.

Finally, after days of painstakingly laboring over each detail, the barristers presented her with the weighty document and sixteen copies. All she had to do to consummate the project was sign, as they said, her "John Henry."

The great lady signed. Sighing a collective sigh of relief, the lawyers left to catch their respective planes heading throughout the country.

One of the attorneys made it as far as Miami before frantically calling his lady client and winging back to Nassau. Other calls, other lawyers followed through day and night.

The trouble? The dear old one had signed just as she had been told: "John Henry."

My years of calling a vineyard home will never be forgotten. They can't be relived but, then, who really wants a rerun of a fantastic memory?

I only insist on getting in the last word.

Omar never said it; but I do. Love and kisses to the wine people!

A NOTE ABOUT THE AUTHOR

Mary Lester is the most widely read woman wine writer in the world today. Her internationally popular newspaper column, "Wine Diggity," distributed by *Copley News Service*, runs in over two hundred newspapers coast to coast besides Japan, Canada and Brazil. She is the wine columnist for *Teacher's Lounge* Magazine, contributes wine features to other publications and frequently "ghosts" articles for newspapers and magazines. She is also on the lecture circuit represented by Lola Wilson Celebrities, Beverly Hills, California.

In 1961, the promise of work as a political reporter for the San Francisco *News-Call-Bulletin* brought her to California. But, merely days before starting that job, she was sold on the idea of gambling on the future of wine and becoming America's first woman tour director for a winery and living on a vineyard.

Miss Lester, dubbed "America's First Lady of Premium Wines," relates her adventurous experiences during a decade as tour director, resident hostess and public relations representative for the world famous Almadén Vineyards in Los Gatos, California. She was the only woman in the world to serve in such a capacity.

She has personally entertained over 250,000 people, talked before wine makers, retailers, restaurant owners and food editors. She has compared notes on wine with members of the Royal Family of England as well as other members of royalty in Europe. Miss Lester has also guested on national and local TV and radio and stumped the panel on *To Tell the Truth* where she was the "real" Mary Lester.

One of the handful of women voted a member of the exclusive American Society of Enologists, Miss Lester enthusiastically keeps up with the latest happenings on the wine scene. Many wine makers believe she has a more diversified understanding of what the public wants from the wine industry, needs, and will get, than probably any other woman in America today.

A winner of the 1972 national Wine and Health Writing Awards contest, she also received acclaim by the Oregon Wine Growers' Association when they gave her their "Corker of the Year" award in recognition of her promoting wines.

In *Hand Me That Corkscrew, Bacchus* Miss Lester writes and speaks as an honest, humorous, warm human being — opening her arms and personality to the thousands and thousands of visitors she personally entertained. "It was always a hectic, unexpected, ninety to one hundred-hour week, but the champagne enabled me to love almost every minute of it!"

Typesetting by Workman Service, Inc., Minneapolis, Minnesota